The Times-Picayune

THANK YOU, BOYS

A SALUTE TO THE SAINTS

Having turned the NFL upside down with their play during the 2006 season, the Saints and Reggie Bush — scoring on an 88-yard touchdown catch from Drew Brees against the Bears in the NFC championship game — took fans on an awe-inspiring ride.

STAFF PHOTO BY SCOTT THRELKELD

The Times-Picayune

Designed by Adrianna Garcia
Edited by Michael J. Montalbano and Richard Russell
Photo editing by Doug Parker

Additional design: Tiffany Bennett Leashore

Photographers: Chuck Cook, Rusty Costanza, Michael DeMocker, Brett Duke, Chris Granger, Ted Jackson, Eliot Kamenitz, John McCusker, Susan Poag, Matt Rose, Scott Threlkeld

Contributing writers: John DeShazier, Peter Finney, Chris Rose, Jimmy Smith, Mike Triplett

Sports editor: Doug Tatum

Assistant sports editor: Kevin Spain

Design director: George Berke

Assistant photo editors: G. Andrew Boyd, David Grunfeld, Dinah Rogers, Robert Steiner

Photo imaging: Joseph Graham, Alexander Maillho

Dan Shea, Managing Editor/News

Sports Publishing LLC

Publisher: Peter L. Bannon
Senior managing editors: Susan M. Moyer and Joseph J. Bannon Jr.
Coordinating editor: Noah A. Amstadter
Art director: K. Jeffrey Higgerson

ISBN: 978-1-59670-275-2

Cover photo by Rusty Costanza. Back cover illustration by Tony O. Champagne.

THEN

AUG. 31, 2005
Two days after Hurricane Katrina brought its wrath upon the Crescent City, a tattered Superdome — home to six Super Bowls — had become a symbol of despair following the greatest disaster in U.S. history. Thousands of people flocked to the Superdome as a shelter of last resort, but heartbreak and misery followed them as the roof tore off and the rain poured in. The Saints became a nomadic team, and they didn't play a home game at the Superdome for the next 13 months.

STAFF PHOTO BY TED JACKSON

4

SEPTEMBER 2006

NFL Commissioner Paul Tagliabue insisted the Saints return to the Superdome following Hurricane Katrina, and with New Orleans still making incremental strides, the re-opening of the Superdome became a beacon of what was achievable – and gave Tagliabue reason to smile.

NOW

The season of the Saints

A 3-13 record. A Superdome shattered by Katrina. A fan base scattered by floodwaters. And a team, many thought, was on the verge of permanently leaving town. At the end of 2005 there was little optimism that a city in need of good news would find it in the New Orleans Saints. Then it happened. A new coach. A new quarterback. A Heisman Trophy winning draft pick. It all produced magic on the field. In getting to the NFC championship game, the 2006 Saints did more than just set a new franchise standard. They provided hope and happiness for people who desperately needed it. And discovered that Cinderella stories aren't just fairy tales.

Glass cleat designed and made by James Vella of Vella Vetro of New Orleans. STAFF PHOTO BY MATT ROSE

The sign says it all. With the game on the line, the Saints' John Carney kicked a 31-yard field goal against the Eagles on the final play of the game Oct. 15, 2006, at the Superdome. More good fortune awaited New Orleans.

STAFF PHOTO BY SCOTT THRELKELD

IT'S GOOD

CONTENTS

SAINTS VS. BROWNS	10
SAINTS VS. PACKERS	16
QUARTERBACK DREW BREES	22
SAINTS VS. FALCONS	26
SAINTS VS. PANTHERS	38
RUNNING BACK REGGIE BUSH	42
SAINTS VS. BUCCANEERS	46
SAINTS VS. EAGLES	52
SAINTS VS. RAVENS	58
RUNNING BACK DEUCE MCALLISTER	62
SAINTS VS. BUCCANEERS (SECOND GAME)	66
SAINTS VS. STEELERS	72
SAINTS VS. BENGALS	76
DEFENSIVE END WILL SMITH	80
SAINTS VS. FALCONS (SECOND GAME)	84
SAINTS VS. 49ERS	90
COACH SEAN PAYTON	96
SAINTS VS. COWBOYS	100
SAINTS VS. REDSKINS	110
SAINTS VS. GIANTS	114
SAINTS VS. PANTHERS (SECOND GAME)	120
SAINTS VS. EAGLES (NFC DIVISIONAL PLAYOFF GAME)	128
SAINTS VS. BEARS (NFC CHAMPIONSHIP GAME)	140
TRAINING CAMP	146
NFL FINAL STANDINGS	150
SAINTS STATISTICS 151 (INDIVIDUAL, TEAM)	151
ROSTER	152
HONORS AND AWARDS	153
FOUR HORSEMEN	154
THROUGH THE YEARS	155
COMPLETE SCORECARD	156

Marques Colston, a seventh-round draft pick from Hofstra, gives the extra effort and scores on a 12-yard pass from Drew Brees during the third quarter against the Cleveland Browns. Colston raised some eyebrows by catching four passes for 49 yards as the Saints started on a winning note. STAFF PHOTO BY SCOTT THRELKELD

CLEVELAND Browns

19

14

A FINE START

Young players deliver like veterans in Sean Payton's debut as the Saints head coach

BY JIMMY SMITH Staff writer

In the sink-or-swim world of the NFL, the Saints had an opportunity on Week 1 to remain buoyant or plummet to the bottom of adjacent Lake Erie.

It fell to the most inexperienced individuals on the roster, including their leader, to stay afloat against the Cleveland Browns in the regular-season opener.

That the Saints beat the Browns 19-14 before an announced crowd of 72,915 at Cleveland Browns Stadium was a testament to the performance of a handful of players and one head coach who were making their pro football debuts — literally or figuratively.

"What was encouraging today was we had about four or five young players all of a sudden stepping up and getting their feet wet. Not dipping their toe in the water. But jumping in," first-year Coach Sean Payton said. "(Third-year receiver) Devery Henderson was one of those young guys. Marques Colston. Jahri Evans. Reggie Bush. Roman Harper. These are all first-year guys."

It went deeper than that, though.

Consider that the Saints' offensive line featured a rookie right guard in Evans, a right tackle (Jon Stinchcomb) who had played in 10 games during his four-year career, a left tackle (Jammal Brown) starting at the position for the first time, a new center (Jeff Faine) and a new left guard (Jamar Nesbit) that didn't allow a sack of Drew Brees while consistently opening holes for tailbacks Bush and Deuce McAllister.

Consider that Payton lost his two fullbacks, Mike Karney (right calf strain) and Keith Joseph (right knee strain) about one quarter into the game and had to modify his offensive game plan accordingly.

Consider that rookie strong safety Harper had a key sack of Cleveland's Charlie Frye late in the fourth quarter that forced a punt as the Saints nursed a five-point lead, and that safety Josh Bullocks, in his second season, squashed the Browns' last-ditch drive by intercepting a Frye pass that ricocheted off the fingers of intended receiver Braylon Edwards at New Orleans' 30-yard line with 1:43 remaining.

Scott Fujita, New Orleans' marquee defensive free-agent acquisition during the offseason, celebrates after he caused a fumble in the second quarter against Cleveland.

STAFF PHOTO BY SCOTT THRELKELD

12

SAINTS 19 | BROWNS 14

"There were a couple of plays that were frustrating, but by and large, our focus and effort, I'm proud of the way these guys played, proud of their effort," Payton said.

After losing Karney and Joseph, Payton adjusted his play-calling and kept the Browns off balance with a variety of formations — lining up Bush as a split end, a flanker in the slot, or a single back in the backfield; an empty backfield with Brees under center; a formation that featured three wide receivers on one side of the line; another that had two tight ends, two wideouts and one back; one, on a third down, that had Bush, Colston and tight end Ernie Conwell in the backfield that resulted in a quick pass to Bush for a first down.

"You want to have a balanced attack," said Brees, who was 17 of 31 for 176 yards and one touchdown (a 12-yarder to Colston in the third quarter). "We got in a situation where we didn't have any fullbacks, and we were having to work tight ends in at fullback and do some creative things with motioning them around. The offensive line did a great job in pass protection and the run game. It was pretty much 5 yards a pop in the run game. You can't complain about that."

Yet it was Bush's versatility that enabled the Saints to diversify their offensive looks and keep the Browns guessing just how or where Bush would get his hands on the ball.

Bush finished with 119 — 61 on 14 carries, 58 on eight receptions — of the Saints' 326 yards of total offense. He also had 22 yards on three punt returns.

On the Saints' first scoring drive that culminated in the longest of John Carney's four field goals (43, 25, 21 and 20 yards), Bush caught a key third-down pass for 11 yards, and on the second field-goal drive his 18-yard dash up the middle moved the ball to Cleveland's 24. On the Saints' only touchdown drive, Bush caught a key third-down pass for 14 yards and accounted for 37 of the drive's 73 yards.

Defensively, the Saints limited the Browns to 85 rushing yards (Frye had 44 of those on scrambles when he was flushed from the pocket), sacked Frye five times and forced a fumble. Cleveland finished with 186 total yards.

"A lot of guys made plays today," Bush said. "I don't think anybody played like a rookie."

TEAM	1ST	2ND	3RD	4TH	FINAL
SAINTS	3	6	7	3	19
BROWNS	0	0	7	7	14

ATTENDANCE — 72,915 AT CLEVELAND BROWNS STADIUM

SCORING SUMMARY

SAINTS — John Carney 43-yard field goal. Ten plays, 27 yards in 9:37.

SAINTS — Carney 25-yard field goal. Twelve plays, 73 in 14:28.

SAINTS — Carney 21-yard field goal. Nine plays, 30 yards in 8:25.

BROWNS — Kellen Winslow 18-yard pass from Charlie Frye (Phil Dawson kick). Ten plays, 67 yards in 9:05.

SAINTS — Marques Colston 12-yard pass from Drew Brees (Carney kick). Eleven plays, 73 yards in 2:00.

BROWNS — Frye 1-yard run. (Dawson kick). Thirteen plays, 74 yards in 11:20.

SAINTS — Carney 20-yard field goal. Eleven plays, 70 yards in 5:42.

TEAM STATISTICS

TEAM STATISTICS	SAINTS	BROWNS
FIRST DOWNS	17	15
RUSHES-YARDS (NET)	40-150	22-85
PASSING YARDS (NET)	176	101
PASSES (ATT-COMP-INT)	17-31-1	16-27-2
TOTAL OFFENSIVE PLAYS-YARDS	71-326	54-186
FUMBLES-LOST	1-1	1-1
PUNTS (NUMBER-AVG)	3-45.0	6-44.2
PUNT RETURNS-YARDS	3-22	2-41
KICKOFF RETURNS-YARDS	1-27	5-114
PENALTY YARDS	6-44	4-35
POSSESSION TIME	32:46	27:14
SACKED (YARDS LOST)	0-0	5-31
FIELD GOALS (ATT-MADE)	4-4	0-0

INDIVIDUAL OFFENSIVE STATISTICS

RUSHING — SAINTS — Deuce McAllister 22-90; Reggie Bush 14-61; Mike Karney 1-1; Drew Brees 3-2.
BROWNS — Charlie Frye 6-44; Reuben Droughns 11-27; Jerome Harrison 2-14; Terrelle Smith 1-0; Lawrence Vickers 2-0.

PASSING — SAINTS — Drew Brees 17/31-1-1, 176. BROWNS — Charlie Frye 16/27-1-2, 132.

RECEIVING — SAINTS — Reggie Bush 8-58; Marques Colston 4-49; Devery Henderson 3-44; Joe Horn 2-25.
BROWNS — Kellen Winslow 8-63; Dennis Northcutt 4-37; Braylon Edwards 2-23; Steve Heiden 1-7; Terrelle Smith 1-2.

INDIVIDUAL DEFENSIVE STATISTICS

INTERCEPTIONS — SAINTS — Josh Bullocks 1; Scott Fujita 1.
BROWNS — Sean Jones 1.

SACKS — SAINTS — Brian Young 3; Roman Harper 1; Will Smith 1.
BROWNS — none.

TACKLES — SAINTS — Josh Bullocks 5-1; Roman Harper 5-0; Mike McKenzie 5-1; Scott Fujita 4-2; Scott Shanle 4-2; Brian Young 4-1; Will Smith 3-2; Fred Thomas 3-1.
BROWNS — Andra Davis 9-3; D'Qwell Jackson 7-3; Leigh Bodden 6-0; Gary Baxter 4-1; Brian Russell 4-1.

 WEEK 1 | SAINTS 19 VS. BROWNS 14 | FALCONS 20 VS. PANTHERS 6 | RAVENS 27 VS. BUCCANEERS 0

GAME 1 | SEPTEMBER 10, 2006 | CLEVELAND BROWNS STADIUM

SAINTS 19 | BROWNS 14

John Carney finds the going crowded, but he connects on a 20-yard field goal in the fourth quarter against the Browns. Carney kicked four field goals (45, 25, 21) as New Orleans held off Cleveland.

STAFF PHOTO BY SCOTT THRELKELD

 SAINTS 1-0   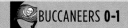 FALCONS 1-0   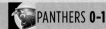 BUCCANEERS 0-1   PANTHERS 0-1   WEEK 1 | **NFC SOUTH**

15

New Orleans fell to Green Bay 52-3 during the 2005 season, but running back Deuce McAllister and the Saints reversed their fortunes and fended off the Packers this time around.

STAFF PHOTO BY SUSAN POAG

GREEN BAY **Packers**

34

27

SAY CHEESE

After faltering early against Green Bay, New Orleans is all smiles by the end

BY MIKE TRIPLETT Staff writer

About 30 minutes after his team did the unthinkable, coming from behind to win at Green Bay 34-27 and start the season 2-0, Saints Coach Sean Payton tried to do the impossible.

He tried to downplay the Sept. 25 return to the Superdome against the division rival Atlanta Falcons, also off to a 2-0 start.

"Hey, it's the third week of the season," Payton said of the upcoming Week 3 game in New Orleans. "You guys are going to start feeding these guys a bunch of cheese and everything else. But this is the third game of the season. That's what it is."

With all due respect to the rookie head coach, there was no use trying to stop the momentum.

The Saints won for the first time in three trips to Lambeau Field — and they did it by coming back from a 13-0 deficit — their biggest comeback victory since 2003.

"Man, you'll go a long time before you see another win after you turn the ball over three times like that in the first quarter on the road," Payton said. "We talked about ebb and flow and momentum changes on the road and being able to battle through some of the adversity. Now, we weren't counting on that type of adversity, and hopefully we won't have to for a while."

The Saints came back to take a 14-13 halftime lead, then hung on for a victory when Packers gunslinger Brett Favre ran out of bullets in the final minutes, throwing incomplete on four consecutive passes from the Saints' 44-yard line.

Drew Brees, who played the role of gunslinger himself, finished with 353 yards passing — 11th best in team history — going 26-of-41 with two touchdowns.

Brees threw one interception and lost two fumbles, all on the Saints' first three possessions.

"That's tough on three consecutive drives to shoot yourself in the foot like that and get down 13-0," Brees said. "But I think for us just to hang in there, it showed a lot of faith, just to believe that things were going to turn around, good things were going to start to happen.

"You know, I feel like as an offense we have a lot of

The Packers found success on offense in the first half, but Will Smith — celebrating a turnover in the third quarter — and the Saints made big plays when it mattered most down the stretch.

STAFF PHOTO BY SUSAN POAG

18

SAINTS 34 | PACKERS 27

confidence when we're out there. We have that attitude like, if they stop us one time or they get a turnover, 'Hey, they got lucky. Next time out, we're going to walk down the field and score.'

"I think we're building that, and I think we're going to continue to build that."

Things couldn't have started much worse for the Saints, who came into Green Bay as unexpected favorite after a Week 1 victory at Cleveland.

On the third play of the game, Brees cocked to throw deep, but the ball was stripped by defensive end Aaron Kampman. Favre followed with a touchdown pass to rookie receiver Greg Jennings for a 7-0 lead.

On the Saints' next possession, Brees again was sacked and stripped of the ball, this time by defensive end Kabeer Gbaja-Biamila.

And on the Saints' third possession, Brees was intercepted when he "guessed wrong" and threw a deep ball that receiver Devery Henderson wasn't expecting.

By that time, Green Bay led 13-0 — but then Brees got going.

He completed 10 of 13 passes for 119 yards on two touchdown drives before halftime — the first a 3-yard run by Deuce McAllister, the next a 26-yard pass to Henderson.

The game continued to ebb and flow in the second half.

John Carney kicked two field goals to give the Saints a 20-13 lead. Favre threw a touchdown pass to Robert Ferguson. Brees threw a 35-yard touchdown pass to rookie Marques Colston, who used his large frame to box out safety Nick Collins. McAllister ran one in from 23 yards after a Packers fumble, and Favre threw a 6-yard touchdown pass to Noah Herron with 4:18 remaining — the last score of the game.

"I thought the defense did a heck of a job," Brees said of a unit that forced two turnovers — including safety Omar Stoutmire's crucial interception in the end zone to halt a long Packers drive early in the third quarter. "We had a stint there where we were just feeding off each other."

Favre finished 31-of-55 for 340 yards, three touchdowns and one interception.

Saints receiver Joe Horn had five catches for 88 yards, including a 57-yarder that set up a field goal in the third quarter. Rookie tailback Reggie Bush caught eight passes for 68 yards as eight Saints receivers caught passes.

TEAM	1ST	2ND	3RD	4TH	FINAL
SAINTS	0	14	6	14	34
PACKERS	13	0	0	14	27
ATTENDANCE				70,602 AT LAMBEAU FIELD	

SCORING SUMMARY

PACKERS **Greg Jennings 22-yard pass from Brett Favre (Dave Rayner kick). Five plays, 37 yards in 2:36.**

PACKERS **Rayner 24-yard field goal. Four plays, 9 yards in 0:58.**

PACKERS **Rayner 36-yard field goal. Eight plays, 75 yards in 3:53.**

SAINTS **Deuce McAllister 3-yard run (John Carney kick). Nine plays, 58 yards in 3:25.**

SAINTS **Devery Henderson 26-yard pass from Drew Brees (Carney kick). Ten plays, 73 yards in 3:31.**

SAINTS **Carney 45-yard field goal. Five plays, 53 yards in 2:06.**

SAINTS **Carney 47-yard field goal. Five plays, 30 yards in 1:22.**

PACKERS **Robert Ferguson 4-yard pass from Favre (Rayner kick). Nine plays, 80 yards in 3:44.**

SAINTS **Marques Colston 35-yard pass from Brees (Carney kick). Six plays, 65 yards in 2:27.**

SAINTS **McAllister 23-yard run (Carney kick). One play, 23 yards in 0:07.**

PACKERS **Noah Herron 6-yard pass from Favre (Rayner kick). Ten plays, 68 yards in 3:36.**

TEAM STATISTICS

TEAM STATISTICS	SAINTS	PACKERS
FIRST DOWNS	20	21
RUSHES-YARDS (NET)	22-48	20-63
PASSING YARDS (NET)	332	322
PASSES (ATT-COMP-INT)	26-41-1	31-55-1
TOTAL OFFENSIVE PLAYS-YARDS	67-380	77-385
FUMBLES-LOST	4-2	2-1
PUNTS (NUMBER-AVG)	4-46.5	6-47.7
PUNT RETURNS-YARDS	6-64	3-10
KICKOFF RETURNS-YARDS	3-59	5-101
PENALTY YARDS	2-14	5-31
POSSESSION TIME	28:04	31:56
SACKED (YARDS LOST)	4-21	2-18
FIELD GOALS (ATT-MADE)	2-2	2-2

INDIVIDUAL OFFENSIVE STATISTICS

RUSHING **SAINTS — Deuce McAllister 12-47; Reggie Bush 6-5; Drew Brees 4-4. PACKERS — Ahman Green 16-42; Donald Driver 1-16; Noah Herron 3-5.**

PASSING **SAINTS — Drew Brees 26/41-2-1, 353. PACKERS — Brett Favre 31/55-3-1, 340.**

RECEIVING **SAINTS — Joe Horn 5-88; Reggie Bush 8-68; Marques Colston 4-58; Devery Henderson 3-51; Mark Campbell 1-33; Deuce McAllister 1-24. PACKERS — Donald Driver 8-153; Greg Jennings 6-67; Ahman Green 6-48; David Martin 6-44; Bubba Franks 3-18; Noah Herron 1-6.**

INDIVIDUAL DEFENSIVE STATISTICS

INTERCEPTIONS **SAINTS — Omar Stoutmire 1. Packers. — Al Harris 1.**

SACKS **SAINTS — Will Smith 1; Willie Whitehead 1. PACKERS — Aaron Kampman 3; Kabeer Gbaja-Biamila 1.**

TACKLES **SAINTS — Jason Craft 7-0; Roman Harper 6-1; Scott Fujita 4-4; Scott Shanle 4-3; Mike McKenzie 3-0; Will Smith 3-0. PACKERS — Nick Collins 8-0; A.J. Hawk 7-0; Marquand Manuel 6-0; Charles Woodson 6-1; Aaron Kampman 4-0; Donald Lee 4-0.**

SAINTS 34 | PACKERS 27

With the game up for grabs, safety Omar Stoutmire intercepts a pass intended for Green Bay fullback William Henderson deep in Saints' territory early in the third quarter.

STAFF PHOTO BY SUSAN POAG

 SAINTS 2-0 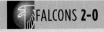 FALCONS 2-0 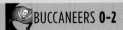 BUCCANEERS 0-2  PANTHERS 0-2 WEEK 2 | **NFC SOUTH**

21

#9

DREW BREES

DREW CHRISTOPHER BREES

born	JANUARY 15, 1979
birthplace	AUSTIN, TEXAS
attended	WESTLAKE HIGH SCHOOL
	PURDUE UNIVERSITY
position	QUARTERBACK
height	6 FEET
weight	209 POUNDS
nfl experience	SIX SEASONS

23

DREW BREES

Quarterback shows leadership and passes with honors

The Saints got their man.

New Orleans agreed to terms with free-agent quarterback Drew Brees on a six-year, $60 million deal March, 14, 2006, including a guaranteed $10 million in the first year.

The Saints made it happen by showing Brees the love — and the money — outbidding all other teams for his services. The Saints owed Brees another $12 million bonus in March 2007 if they wanted to keep him on the roster.

Chances are, they will, especially after he led the Saints to the NFC championship game and landed himself a spot in the Pro Bowl.

"Really, what it came down to was who I felt like believed in me the most," said Brees, who tore the labrum on his right, throwing shoulder while trying to recover a fumble in his final game with the San Diego Chargers during Week 17 of the 2005 regular season. "I really got a great feeling from the Saints organization and the head coach, and I really felt like I have the opportunity to do something great here.

"The Saints have made it clear from the beginning that I'm their guy they want to build this thing with, and that's really exciting."

Funny as it sounded, Brees was looking forward to getting hit in the Saints' first preseason game against the Tennessee Titans on Sept. 12, 2006, in Jackson, Miss.

"That sounds crazy," he said. "But there's definitely a difference between standing there in practice and obviously taking live bullets in a game (for the first time since getting injured) and getting hit and thrown down on that shoulder."

Brees was excited about his recovery — his arm strength, the flexibility, the lack of soreness and swelling.

"I can tell you, when I'm out there, I don't think about my shoulder at all," Brees said.

When New Orleans ended a two-game home losing streak and his personal streak of five consecutive 300-yard passing games came to an end against the San Francisco 49ers in the Saints' 34-10 victory Dec. 3, 2006, at the Superdome, Brees was quick to compliment his teammates.

"I've told you guys this in the past: With this offense, you never know whose day it's going to be," Brees said. "Today, it was the running game and Reggie (Bush) and Deuce (McAllister)."

Humble, and the ultimate team player. That described Brees.

After he was chosen to the Pro Bowl, Brees deflected the praise to his teammates.

"This is a tremendous honor to be named to the team; it just makes it a special year here," Brees said. "It was one of my goals coming into the season, personally. To be named the starter, to represent our conference is a large responsibility. I wouldn't be here without the efforts of the guys on my team and what we have been able to accomplish this year."

— MIKE TRIPLETT

CAREER PASSING STATISTICS

SEASON	TEAM	GAMES	STARTS	PASSES	COMPLETIONS	PERCENTAGE	YARDS	LONG	TD	INT
2001	Chargers	1	0	27	15	55.6	221	40	1	0
2002	Chargers	16	16	526	320	60.8	3,284	52	17	16
2003	Chargers	11	11	356	205	57.6	2,108	68	11	15
2004	Chargers	15	15	400	262	65.5	3,159	79	27	7
2005	Chargers	16	16	500	323	64.6	3,576	54	24	15
2006	Saints	16	16	554	356	64.3	4,418	86	26	11

POSTSEASON PASSING STATISTICS

SEASON	TEAM	GAMES	STARTS	PASSES	COMPLETIONS	PERCENTAGE	YARDS	LONG	TD	INT
2004	Chargers	1	1	42	31	73.8	319	44	2	1
2006	Saints	2	2	47	81	58.0	597	88	3	1

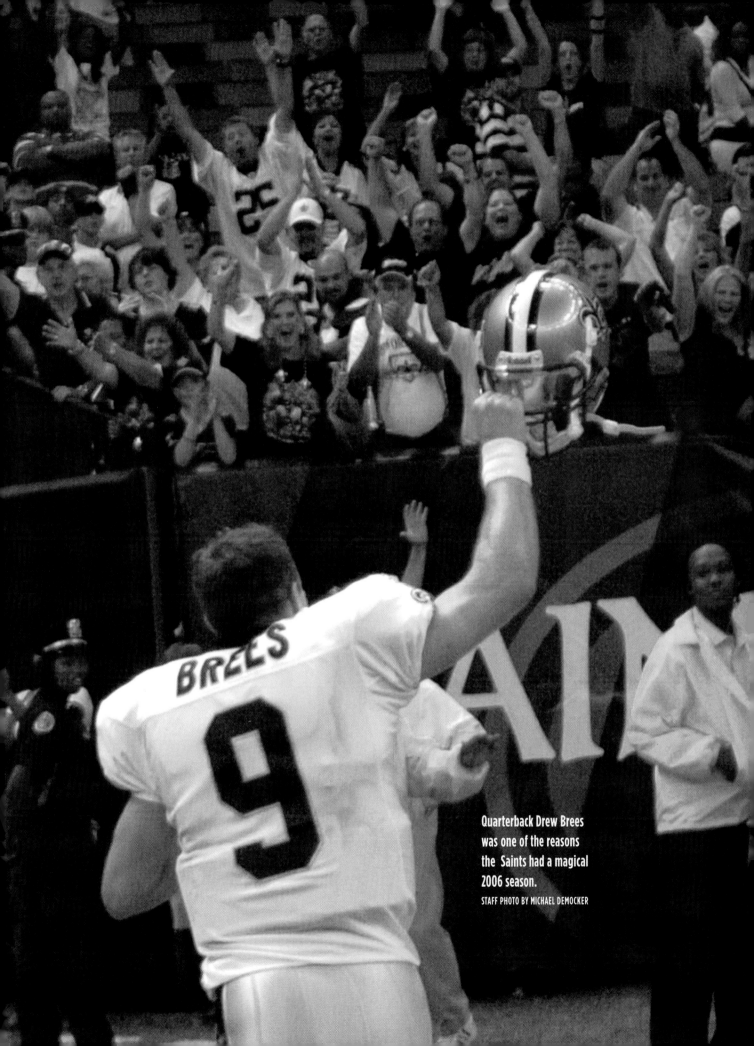

Quarterback Drew Brees
was one of the reasons
the Saints had a magical
2006 season.
STAFF PHOTO BY MICHAEL DEMOCKER

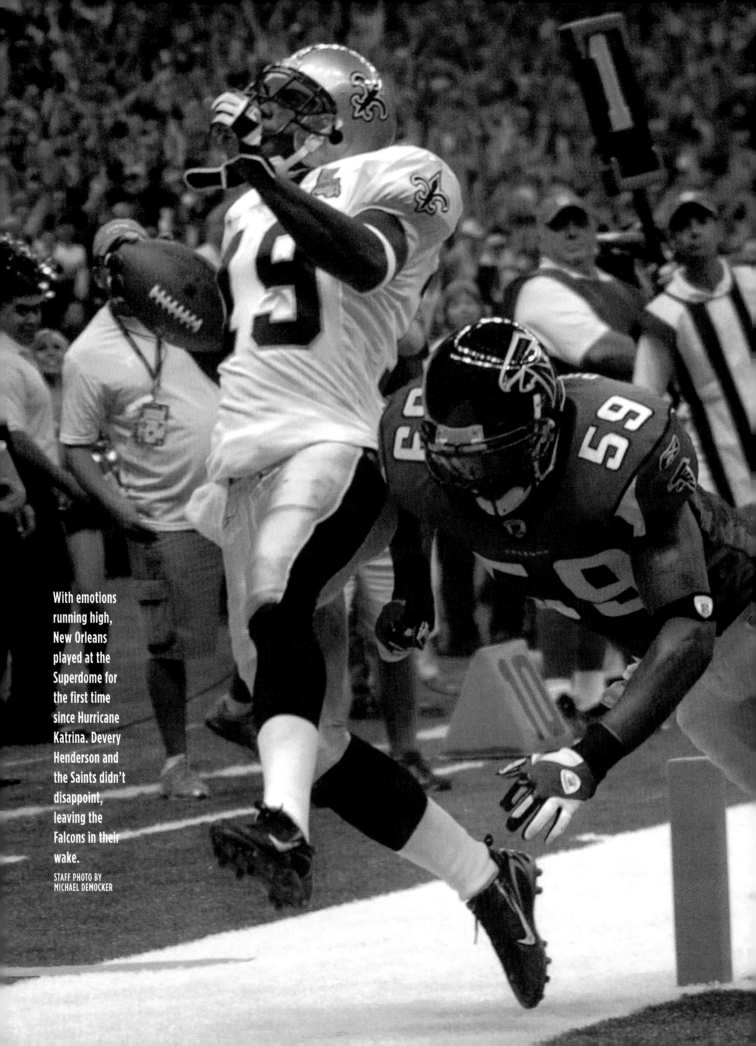

With emotions running high, New Orleans played at the Superdome for the first time since Hurricane Katrina. Devery Henderson and the Saints didn't disappoint, leaving the Falcons in their wake.

STAFF PHOTO BY MICHAEL DEMOCKER

ATLANTA **Falcons**

23

3

PERFECT STORM

This time the Falcons — not the Saints — fell the wrath of a powerful force

BY JIMMY SMITH Staff writer

The forces of nature had brought New Orleans to its knees a little more than a year ago, but its football team brought a still-teetering region to its feet Monday night.

And the afterglow of a resounding 23-3 nationally-televised victory over the Atlanta Falcons not only put the Saints atop the NFC South with a 3-0 record, but quite possibly shook all of New Orleans out of it's post-Katrina funk and placed it on a clear path toward its ultimate renaissance.

The Saints' easily dispatched the Atlanta Falcons in front of a sellout crowd of 70,003 in an emotional return to the once-tattered Superdome that left Coach Sean Payton hand-slapping fans rimming the West side of the Plaza level and owner Tom Benson doing his postgame boogie once again to the strains of Fats Domino singing "When The Saints Go Marchin' In."

It was the ending for which so many had hoped: their beloved team playing once again in a renovated Dome, last year the site of so much human tragedy in the face of a killer storm that obliterated levees, inundated the city and left more than a thousand dead.

And walking out with a victory.

"We dedicated the game all to the City of New Orleans," linebacker Scott Fujita said. "It was well-deserved."

If ever a game exemplified contributions from each phase in victory, it was Monday night's.

The Saints' offensive play calling left Atlanta's defense, which had allowed opponents a little more than 50 rushing yards per game, often befuddled. New Orleans ran for 146 yards on 34 carries, a 4.3 average — led by Deuce McAllister's 81 yards on 19 carries, and Reggie Bush's 53 on 13.

"When we were able to run inside early, they brought the safety up — and we were able to do all kinds of things," McAllister said.

New Orleans' defense limited Atlanta — the league's best rushing offense — to 117 yards — 57 from quarterback Michael Vick and 44 from Warrick Dunn. The Saints sacked Vick five times, allowed the Falcons 10 first downs and gave up only a 26-yard field goal by

With a national television audience watching, Atlanta's Warrick Dunn is running on empty against Saints defensive tackle Rodney Leisle and company.

STAFF PHOTO BY MATT ROSE

28

SAINTS 23 | FALCONS 3

SAINTS 23 | FALCONS 3

Morten Andersen.

"All we cared about was stopping the run," Saints defensive end Will Smith said. "Play the run first. Play the pass second."

Vick finished 12-for-31 for 137 yards. Smith said the Saints saw the way Atlanta's first two opponents — Carolina and Tampa Bay — had defended Vick.

"They were rushing him like a normal quarterback," Smith said. "Michael Vick is not a normal quarterback."

The Saints' special teams blocked a punt, which resulted in a touchdown, and blocked an Andersen field-goal attempt with less than two minutes remaining in the first half — setting up a 1:46 drive that was highlighted by a back-breaking 51-yard field goal by John Carney on the final play of the half that pushed the Saints' lead to 20-3.

Yet it was the play of New Orleans's defense that set the tone against Atlanta.

"The defensive line was outstanding," said Fujita, who had the first sack of Vick. "The way they shut down the inside run and controlling the edges against a guy like Vick was critical."

When Payton spoke earlier in the week about how special it would be to win Monday night's game, he wasn't referring to the Saints' special team's unit.

But it was just that facet of the team that got New Orleans off to a rousing start in the first quarter.

Following Fujita's sack of Vick on third-and-4 from Atlanta's 35-yard line, the Falcons were forced to punt.

Safety Steve Gleason stunted around a teammate, came cleanly up the middle and got two hands on a punt by Michael Koenen. Cornerback Curtis Deloatch fell on the football for a touchdown as it trickled into the South end zone, and the already frenzied crowd went berserk, as did Payton who ran up the sideline pumping his fist in an uppercut motion.

It was the first punch to the Falcons' collective jaws.

And it wasn't the last.

"I think the most important thing is that my goal was to come out and play my ass off for the city of New Orleans, my team, and all the people who have been here and gone through everything we've gone through," Gleason said. "Most people don't understand what we've been through down here."

Said Vick said, referring to the Saints' defense. "That storm was tough. That was Katrina over there."

Curtis Deloatch and the spirits of fans in the Crescent City soar after he picked up a blocked punt by Steve Gleason against the Falcons early in the first quarter.

STAFF PHOTO BY MICHAEL DEMOCKER

Before the start of the Saints-Falcons game at the Superdome, fans partied as if it were Fat Tuesday. STAFF PHOTO BY MATT ROSE

With the Saints poised to take the field, the crowd rose to its feet and made their presence felt. STAFF PHOTO BY RUSTY COSTANZA

SAINTS 23 | FALCONS 3

Outside the Superdome, fans counted down the final moments before they were allowed to enter the building. STAFF PHOTO BY TED JACKSON.

33

Cheers & tears

EMOTIONAL HOMECOMING FUELS
NEW ORLEANS FANS AND PLAYERS

John DeShazier

The perfect end to this day in New Orleans would've been the mass reconstruction of thousands of homes, the go-ahead given for hundreds of thousands of still-displaced citizens to come home, the vow to return by 95 percent of the businesses that closed up shop or left town and sprang up somewhere else after Katrina.

But for Saints fans, watching the Saints plant a cleat squarely in the Atlanta Falcons' rear end was a pretty satisfying substitute.

Nearly lost amid the clutter of a week's worth of hoopla and enough pregame grandiosity to rival a Super Bowl was the fact that there still was a football game to be played. The Saints, thank goodness, didn't let that minor detail escape their attention.

Instead, they plugged into their electrified home crowd and earned every drop of affection they were showered with in their first regular-season game at the Superdome since Dec. 26, 2004. And they continued to defy expectations this season, running their record to 3-0 for the first time since 2002 with a 23-3 victory over the Falcons.

A year after finishing 3-13, the Saints now are spreading the gospel, creating believers from a fan base and city looking for someone, and something, to believe in.

"It's the loudest I've ever heard it in pregame warm-ups," New Orleans defensive end Will Smith said. "I don't think anyone went to work today."

The day had a holiday feel to it, and, obviously, it was easy to fall into a trap and make more of the game than it was — to somehow link New Orleans' recovery to the rebound of the Saints and the reopening of the Superdome. And that was a colossal mistake because while one entity sparkles, the other continued to rest in its squalor, a national eyesore that deserved headline display until the repair work was commissioned and done.

But for a region that needed to scream — something other than the vitriol spewed at FEMA, insurance adjusters and the state's Road Home program — the Saints gave a good reason to yell.

And laugh. And cry.

The latter of which grown men did while the Saints

With the Superdome rocking — U2 and Green Day had revved up an already jazzed crowd — the Saints take the field and proceed to roll over the Falcons.

SAINTS 23 | FALCONS 3

were announced in pregame introductions.

"I was crying like a baby out there," New Orleans fullback Mike Karney said. "I just got caught up in the moment. I was just so happy for the fans and the people of this city. I had tears in my eyes when I came out on the field. It was just a good feeling to know all 70,000 fans were all there for you."

Said rookie wide receiver Marques Colston: "It was crazy. I felt the stadium moving. It's indescribable the vibe you get when you leave that tunnel."

Once the Saints left it, they never gave fans a reason to sit down or shut up.

The Falcons' first possession ended in a New Orleans touchdown, with Steve Gleason blocking a punt and Curtis Deloatch falling on the ball in the end zone. In the second quarter, nursing a 17-3 lead, the Saints bent enough to allow Atlanta to drive to New Orleans' 2-yard line, sacked Michael Vick and held the Falcons to a field-goal attempt — then blocked Morten Andersen's 25-yard attempt.

When John Carney kicked a 51-yard field goal as time expired in the first half, giving the Saints a 20-3 lead, the lone unknown was where the revelry would commence at the final gun.

Still, it was an odd sensation, this whole business of watching the Saints remain unbeaten after three games. The friendly neighborhood palm reader hadn't foreseen that, not with the Saints making so many off-season changes, not considering it usually took time for a team to gel as well as the Saints apparently had.

But who, more than New Orleanians, deserved to experience a "good" odd?

Fans received "good" kinds of odd relative to how good their football team was. For now, the Saints looked like a good football team.

You had a hard time recalling a more complete paddling administered by the Saints, against anyone. You had a hard time remembering the last time a New Orleans team so thoroughly was fueled by emotion, the screams of fans so thick they seemed to weigh down the Falcons.

But then, this day was destined to be different from the second the NFL said that Sept. 25 would serve as the reopening of the Superdome.

It was special.

"For us, as players, we wanted to win to put the icing on the cake," Saints receiver Joe Horn said.

It wasn't totally perfect, for a city that could stand an injection of perfect. But it was pretty close to it.

TEAM	1ST	2ND	3RD	4TH	FINAL
FALCONS	**3**	**0**	**0**	**0**	**3**
SAINTS	**14**	**6**	**3**	**0**	**23**
ATTENDANCE					70,003 AT THE SUPERDOME

SCORING SUMMARY

SAINTS	Curtis Deloatch blocked-punt return (John Carney kick). 0 yards.
FALCONS	Morten Andersen 26-yard field goal. Nine plays, 65 yards in 3:49.
SAINTS	Devery Henderson 11-yard run (Carney kick). Eight plays, 80 yards in 4:05.
SAINTS	Carney 37-yard field goal. Ten plays, 66 yards in 5:05.
SAINTS	Carney 51-yard field goal. Ten plays, 54 yards in 1:49.
SAINTS	Carney 20-yard field goal. Twelve plays, 73 yards in 7:46.

TEAM STATISTICS	SAINTS	FALCONS
FIRST DOWNS	19	10
RUSHES-YARDS (NET)	34-146	23-117
PASSING YARDS (NET)	180	112
PASSES (ATT-COMP-INT)	20-28-1	12-31-0
TOTAL OFFENSIVE PLAYS-YARDS	63-326	59-229
FUMBLES-LOST	0-0	2-0
PUNTS (NUMBER-AVG)	6-40.8	6-44.2
PUNT RETURNS-YARDS	1-11	4-22
KICKOFF RETURNS-YARDS	2-42	5-137
PENALTY YARDS	4-40	5-43
POSSESSION TIME	32:40	27:20
SACKED (YARDS LOST)	1-11	5-25
FIELD GOALS (ATT-MADE)	3-3	1-2

INDIVIDUAL OFFENSIVE STATISTICS

RUSHING SAINTS — Deuce McAllister 19-81; Reggie Bush 13-53; Devery Henderson 1-11; Drew Brees 1-1.
FALCONS — Michael Vick 6-57; Warrick Dunn 13-44; Justin Griffith 3-16; Jerious Norwood 1-0.

PASSING SAINTS — Drew Brees 20/28-0-0, 191.
FALCONS — Michael Vick 12/31-0-0, 137.

RECEIVING SAINTS — Marques Colston 7-97; Joe Horn 3-47; Reggie Bush 4-19; Devery Henderson 2-15; Deuce McAllister 4-13.
FALCONS — Alge Crumpler 5-49; Ashley Lelie 1-48; Michael Jenkins 2-23; Justin Griffith 2-15; Warrick Dunn 2-2.

INDIVIDUAL DEFENSIVE STATISTICS

INTERCEPTIONS SAINTS — none.
FALCONS — none.

SACKS SAINTS — Scott Fujita 1; Charles Grant 1; Scott Shanle 1; Brian Young 1; Will Smith 1.
FALCONS — Kevin Mathis 1.

TACKLES SAINTS — Scott Fujita 6-2; Josh Bullocks 5-2; Charles Grant 5-0; Mike McKenzie 4-0; Scott Shanle 4-0; Brian Young 4-1.
FALCONS — Michael Boley 9-2; Keith Brooking 8-1; Lawyer Milloy 7-2; Demorrio Williams 7-1; Jason Webster 6-1.

SAINTS 23 | FALCONS 3

Noise inside the Dome hit a crescendo when Steve Gleason blocked the punt of the Falcons' Michael Koenen during the first quarter. STAFF PHOTO BY MICHAEL DEMOCKER

SAINTS 3-0 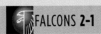FALCONS 2-1 PANTHERS 1-2 BUCCANEERS 0-3 WEEK 3 | **NFC SOUTH**

37

CAROLINA
Panthers

21
18

The Panthers' DeShaun Foster dashes the hopes of the Saints when he eludes Hollis Thomas (99) and Mark Simoneau (53) and scores on a 43-yard run late in the fourth quarter. STAFF PHOTO BY RUSTY COSTANZA

RUN DOWN

With the game on the line, New Orleans lets it slip away against Carolina

BY MIKE TRIPLETT Staff writer

Four quarters into the fourth game of their storybook season, the Saints finally ran out of magic — and their defense finally ran out of steam.

After taking a three-point lead early in the fourth quarter, the Saints couldn't finish off the Carolina Panthers, allowing them to rally for a 21-18 victory on Oct. 1 that closed the gap in the NFC South.

The loss separated the Saints (3-1), Atlanta Falcons (3-1) and Panthers (2-2) in the division race.

"You can't play 3 1/2 quarters of good defense against an offense like this that traditionally does really well in the fourth quarter. They got us today," Saints linebacker Scott Fujita said of the Panthers' offense, which churned out 164 yards on two fourth-quarter touchdown drives to take a 21-10 lead with 1:45 remaining.

The most disheartening play of the Saints' season was just after the two-minute warning, when Panthers tailback DeShaun Foster took a pitch on third-and-7 and escaped down the right sideline for a 43-yard touchdown run.

"Every one of us probably knew what the play was," Fujita said.

The Saints appeared to have several defenders in good position, but linebacker Scott Shanle was the only one to get a hand on Foster, who was tightly guarded by blockers on both sides.

"Most running backs will just go down," Saints defensive end Will Smith said. "But Foster, all day, he kept trying to get that extra yard — and it paid off in the fourth quarter today."

The Saints kept hope alive with an 86-yard touchdown pass from Drew Brees to Marques Colston 30 seconds later, but they failed to recover the onside kick — and for the first time this season they tasted defeat.

"The reality is, they just took advantage of their opportunities more than we did," said Saints tight end Ernie Conwell, who was unable to catch a third-down

John Carney misses a 43-yard field goal attempt just before halftime, one of many opportunities on which New Orleans failed to capitalize on against Carolina.

conversion pass by a matter of inches when the Saints were trailing 14-10 with five minutes remaining.

The Saints missed plenty of chances in the first three quarters, when they had gained nearly 100 yards more than Carolina but trailed 7-3.

New Orleans tailback Reggie Bush lost his first fumble in the NFL at the Panthers' 20-yard line in the second

WEEK 4 | PANTHERS 21 VS. SAINTS 18 | FALCONS 32 VS. CARDINALS 10 | BUCCANEERS, BYE

PANTHERS 21 | SAINTS 18

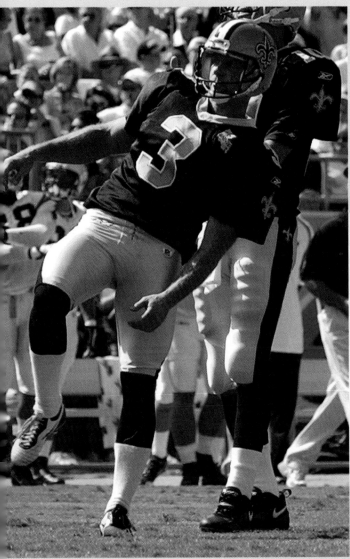

STAFF PHOTO BY RUSTY COSTANZA

TEAM	1ST	2ND	3RD	4TH	FINAL
SAINTS	0	3	0	15	18
PANTHERS	7	0	0	14	21
ATTENDANCE				73,392 AT BANK OF AMERICA STADIUM	

SCORING SUMMARY

PANTHERS Steve Smith 9-yard pass from Jake Delhomme (John Kasay kick). Eight plays, 72 yards in 3:37.

SAINTS John Carney 31-yard field goal. Eleven plays, 68 yards in 6:13.

SAINTS Deuce McAllister 3-yard run (Carney kick). Thirteen plays, 82 yards in 6:49.

PANTHERS Drew Carter 4-yard pass from Delhomme (Kasay kick). Twelve plays, 91 yards in 6:18.

PANTHERS DeShaun Foster 43-yard run (Kasay kick). Seven plays, 73 yards in 3:09.

SAINTS Marques Colston 86-yard pass from Drew Brees (Brees pass to Joe Horn for two-point conversion). Two plays, 76 yards in 0:30.

TEAM STATISTICS

TEAM STATISTICS	SAINTS	PANTHERS
FIRST DOWNS	22	20
RUSHES-YARDS (NET)	23-63	29-167
PASSING YARDS (NET)	344	157
PASSES (ATT-COMP-INT)	28-38-0	19-29-0
TOTAL OFFENSIVE PLAYS-YARDS	62-407	59-324
FUMBLES-LOST	2-1	0-0
PUNTS (NUMBER-AVG)	5-46.0	6-50.7
PUNT RETURNS-YARDS	4-2	2-3
KICKOFF RETURNS-YARDS	4-84	3-56
PENALTY YARDS	5-38	7-48
POSSESSION TIME	29:39	30:21
SACKED (YARDS LOST)	1-5	1-12
FIELD GOALS (ATT-MADE)	1-2	0-0

INDIVIDUAL OFFENSIVE STATISTICS

RUSHING SAINTS — Deuce McAllister 11-39; Reggie Bush 11-22; Drew Brees 1-2. PANTHERS — DeShaun Foster 16-105; DeAngelo Williams 8-62.

PASSING SAINTS — Drew Brees 28/38-1-0, 349. PANTHERS — Jake Delhomme 19/29-2-0, 169.

RECEIVING SAINTS — Marques Colston 5-132; Joe Horn 5-63; Reggie Bush 4-48; Ernie Conwell 5-37; Terrance Copper 2-30; Aaron Stecker 3-15. PANTHERS — Steve Smith 10-87; Keyshawn Johnson 6-63; DeAngelo Williams 1-9; DeShaun Foster 1-6; Drew Carter 1-4.

INDIVIDUAL DEFENSIVE STATISTICS

INTERCEPTIONS SAINTS — none. PANTHERS — none.

SACKS SAINTS — Scott Shanle 1. PANTHERS — Julius Peppers 1.

quarter, and kicker John Carney missed his first field-goal attempt of the season, a 43-yarder just before halftime.

Nevertheless, the Saints took a 10-7 lead on Deuce McAllister's 3-yard touchdown run with 13:33 remaining. That's when Carolina's offense took over.

 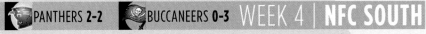

#25

REGGIE BUSH

REGINALD ALFRED BUSH II
born   MARCH 2, 1985
birthplace SPRING VALLEY, CALIFORNIA
attended   HELIX HIGH SCHOOL
UNIVERSITY OF SOUTHERN CALIFORNIA
position   RUNNING BACK
height   6 FEET
weight   203 POUNDS
nfl experience   ROOKIE

REGGIE BUSH

Rookie takes the NFL by storm and proves his worth

The Houston Texans' decision to make North Carolina State defensive end Mario Williams the first overall choice April 29, 2006, gave the Saints a rare opportunity to select the best player available in the draft with the second pick.

And despite listening to trade overtures from the New York Jets, the Saints reveled in their inexplicable good fortune, turned in their card bearing Reggie Bush's name, then accepted universal good wishes for arguably their most popular first-round selection since picking Ole Miss quarterback Archie Manning in the same spot in 1971.

Bush dived into the city with the fervor of a goal-line plunge. He launched himself into several civic activities across the Crescent City, donating to various causes with everything from cash to Hummers to a synthetic turf football field.

But when Bush started to look like a mere mortal on the football field during the 2006 season, he began to experience the same doubts and questions as everyone else who was watching him.

"All the time," said Bush, who finally had the breakout performance everyone was waiting for against the San Francisco 49ers on Dec. 3, 2006, at the Superdome. "Just being in this position that I'm in, I've got a million things going through my head. The constant question to myself is whether I'm doing the right thing. Am I built for this game? All kinds of thoughts.

"But that's just a part of the game, I think. It comes with the territory."

That territory was mostly uncharted. Few rookies, if any, have entered the NFL surrounded by as much hype and hope as Bush, who secured millions of dollars in endorsement deals before he played his first snap.

Through his first 11 games, he was solid, just not spectacular. Then came his four-touchdown performance against the 49ers, in which he sprinted, side-stepped and spun his way to a season-high 168 yards from scrimmage, a throwback to his Heisman Trophy winning days at Southern California.

"I felt like it was a matter of time. I finally felt comfortable. I felt like me," said Bush, who said his rookie season was a "roller coaster."

"I've gone through a lot of ups and downs. But, you know, that's part of the learning process," Bush said. "A lot of people have kind of had this meter for me as to when I'm going to have this breakout game or these huge plays. But obviously, nobody has bigger expectations for me than myself.

"For me, I think this last game lifted a little bit of weight off my shoulders. It just helped me with my confidence level, and it just showed that everything's paying off."

– MIKE TRIPLETT

STAFF PHOTO BY MICHAEL DEMOCKER

RUN, REGGIE, RUN A close-up look at Reggie Bush's season, complete with Saints game results:

	Game 1:	Game 2:	Game 3:	Game 4:	Game 5:	Game 6:	Game 7:	Game 8:	Game 9:	Game 10:	Game 11:
	SAINTS 19	SAINTS 34	SAINTS 23	PANTHERS 21	SAINTS 24	SAINTS 27	RAVENS 35	SAINTS 31	STEELERS 38	BENGALS 31	SAINTS 31
	BROWNS 14	PACKERS 27	FALCONS 3	SAINTS 18	BUCS 21	EAGLES 24	SAINTS 22	BUCS 14	SAINTS 31	SAINTS 16	FALCONS 13
	141 yds	109 yds	72 yds	69 yds	161 yds, 1 TD	89 yds	21 yds	37 yds	96 yds, 1 TD	116 yds	44 yds
	RUSHING: 61	RUSH: 5	RUSH: 53	RUSH: 22	RUSH: 23	RUSH: 25	RUSH: 16	RUSH: -5	RUSH: 49	RUSH: 51	RUSH: 24
	RETURNS: 22	RET: 36	RET: 0	RET: -1	RET: 75	RET: 35	RET: 0	RET: 20	RET: 7	RET: 7	RET: -1
	RECEPTIONS: 58	REC: 68	REC: 19	REC: 48	REC: 63	REC: 29	REC: 5	REC: 22	REC: 40	REC: 58	REC: 21

Rookie Reggie Bush doesn't shy away from making himself accessible to the fans, and he quickly got involved with numerous civic activities.

Game 12:
SAINTS **34**
49ERS **10**

172 yds, 4 TDs

RUSH: 37
RET: 4
REC: 131

Game 13:
SAINTS **42**
COWBOYS **17**

160 yds, 1 TD

RUSH: 37
RET: -2
REC: 125

Game 14:
REDSKINS **16**
SAINTS **10**

46 yds

RUSH: 14
RET: 13
REC: 19

Game 15:
SAINTS **30**
GIANTS **7**

156 yds, 1 TD

RUSH: 126
RET: 7
REC: 23

Game 16:
PANTHERS **31**
SAINTS **21**

33 yds, 1 TD

RUSH: 20
RET: 0
REC: 13

Divisional Playoffs:
SAINTS **27**
EAGLES **24**

95 yds, 1 TD

RUSH: 52
RET: 21
REC: 22

NFC Championship:
BEARS **39**
SAINTS **14**

161 yds, 1 TD

RUSH: 19
RET: 10
REC: 132

TOTAL YARDS
1,779

STAFF GRAPHIC BY DAN SWENSON

TAMPA BAY Buccaneers

24
21

The Buccaneers' Brian Kelly is no match for Saints rookie Reggie Bush, who showed his brilliance running, catching and returning the ball in grand style for the first time as a professional. STAFF PHOTO BY SCOTT THRELKELD

TOUCHDOWN!

Reggie Bush's electrifying first NFL score brings the Saints their fourth victory

BY JIMMY SMITH Staff writer

The investment made 163 days ago yielded the anticipated dividends Oct. 8, 2006.

In startlingly dramatic fashion.

"When you see him on tape in college and you make a decision to draft a player like that, he's a guy who can change games," Saints Coach Sean Payton said. "And today, he changed one."

Reggie Bush's 65-yard fourth-quarter punt return for a touchdown not only snapped his personal professional scoring drought but rallied the Saints to a 24-21 victory over the Tampa Bay Buccaneers at the Superdome in front of a sellout crowd of 68,183.

"It was electrifying," fellow Saints running back Deuce McAllister said.

And it not only helped the Saints overcome a somewhat spotty defensive performance, and avert an upset by a winless Buccaneers team, but it gave the Saints a one-half game NFC South lead over the idle Atlanta Falcons (3-1) and earned New Orleans its fourth victory of the season, one more than all of the storm-altered 2005 season.

When the Saints drafted Bush in the first round of the NFL draft April 29, they envisioned him as a triple-threat player — runner, receiver, return specialist — who was a difference-maker.

Against the Buccaneers, Bush had a professional best 161 all-purpose yards, catching a game-high 11 passes for 63 yards, running nine times for 23 and returning three punts for 75.

His contributions more than offset the fact that Tampa Bay outgained New Orleans 406-314, outrushed the Saints 187-143, despite being the NFL's worst rushing offense heading into the game (43.3 yards per game) and out-passing their opponent 219-171.

"I tip my hat to Reggie Bush," Buccaneers Coach Jon Gruden said. "He made a great play. He lived up to his expectations today. Shame on him."

Tampa Bay was trying to run out the clock and hold on to a 21-17 lead in the game's final five minutes but went three-and-out from its 15-yard line, forcing a Josh Bidwell punt with just more than four

SAINTS 24 | BUCCANEERS 21

With New Orleans needing a score against Tampa Bay, Reggie Bush finds the end zone for the first time as a pro on a 65-yard punt return late in the fourth quarter.

STAFF PHOTO BY MICHAEL DEMOCKER

49

minutes remaining.

Bush fielded the punt, ran right, toward Tampa Bay's sideline, slipped one tackler, turned the corner and, behind blocks from Jason Craft, Steve Gleason and Nate Lawrie, went up the sideline untouched for a score.

"It was one of our basic returns," Lawrie said. "A lot of people got blocks. We set it up great. Reggie did a great job to get to the edge."

The post-touchdown celebration was tempered for a moment while officials sorted out a flag thrown away from the play. But it was a face-mask penalty on Tampa Bay's Torrie Cox, which did not nullify the run.

"I was a little nervous about that flag," Bush said.

No less than one on the Buccaneers' next possession.

Rookie quarterback Bruce Gradkowski, starting his first NFL game in place of injured Chris Simms, was driving Tampa Bay toward another potential game-altering score — he had completed passes of 15 and 18 yards, followed by a 16-yard Carnell "Cadillac" Williams bolt off the left side, when he connected with wide receiver Ike Hilliard with what appeared to be a 38-yard pass to the Saints' 3-yard line.

But back up the field was another penalty flag. Officials had called Buccaneers wide receiver Joey Galloway for offensive pass interference. Galloway had illegally screened off cornerback Jason Craft, which cleared Hilliard's unencumbered route up the sideline.

It was a play the Buccaneers had run previously during the game without penalty.

"But they called it on me on the biggest play of the game," Galloway said.

Tampa Bay ran two more plays but didn't sustain the drive.

McAllister rushed for 123 yards on 15 carries, including a 24-yard touchdown run and a 57-yard rumble that was stopped 3 yards short of the goal line.

Defensive end Charles Grant had a sack of Gradkowski that forced a third-quarter fumble — recovered by Rodney Leisle — which the Saints turned into a 9-yard Drew Brees-to-Ernie Conwell touchdown.

"It's not always going to be perfect," said Brees, pointing out the Saints' anemic 3-for-12 third-down efficiency.

But thanks to the Saints' game-changing draft-day investment, it was another "W" in the bank.

"Reggie made a big play when we needed it," Payton said. "It's about winning games, and style points aren't important. We're 4-1 right now."

TEAM	1ST	2ND	3RD	4TH	FINAL
BUCCANEERS	7	0	7	7	21
SAINTS	3	7	7	7	24
ATTENDANCE				68,183 AT THE SUPERDOME	

SCORING SUMMARY

BUCS Joey Galloway 18-yard pass from Bruce Gradkowski (Matt Bryant kick). Six plays, 61 yards in 3:08.

SAINTS John Carney 21-yard field goal. Eleven plays, 83 yards in 5:04.

SAINTS Deuce McAllister 24-yard run (Carney kick). Ten plays, 88 yards in 4:05.

SAINTS Ernie Conwell 9-yard pass from Drew Brees (Carney kick). Four plays, 25 yards in 1:33.

BUCS Mike Alstott 1-yard run (Bryant kick). Six plays, 74 yards in 3:02.

BUCS Alex Smith 3-yard pass from Gradkowski (Bryant kick). Five plays, 40 yards in 1:46.

SAINTS Reggie Bush 65-yard punt return (Carney kick).

TEAM STATISTICS	SAINTS	BUCCANEERS
FIRST DOWNS	15	18
RUSHES-YARDS (NET)	25-143	33-187
PASSING YARDS (NET)	171	219
PASSES (ATT-COMP-INT)	21-33-0	20-31-0
TOTAL OFFENSIVE PLAYS-YARDS	58-314	66-406
FUMBLES-LOST	0-0	1-1
PUNTS (NUMBER-AVG)	8-44.8	6-38.8
PUNT RETURNS-YARDS	4-78	6-60
KICKOFF RETURNS-YARDS	4-71	4-85
PENALTY YARDS	9-49	8-66
POSSESSION TIME	29:23	30:37
SACKED (YARDS LOST)	0-0	2-6
FIELD GOALS (ATT-MADE)	1-1	0-0

INDIVIDUAL OFFENSIVE STATISTICS

RUSHING **SAINTS** — Deuce McAllister 15-123; Reggie Bush 9-23; Drew Brees 1-minus-3.
BUCCANEERS — Carnell Williams 20-111; Michael Clayton 1-27; Michael Pittman 2-27; Bruce Gradkowski 6-19; Mike Alstott 4-3.

PASSING **SAINTS** — Drew Brees 21/33-1-0, 171.
BUCCANEERS — Bruce Gradkowski 20/31-2-0, 225.

RECEIVING **SAINTS** — Reggie Bush 11-63; Joe Horn 4-48; Marques Colston 3-38; Ernie Conwell 2-14; Deuce McAllister 1-8.
BUCCANEERS — Joey Galloway 4-110; Ike Hilliard 4-34; Michael Pittman 2-31; Alex Smith 5-16; Carnell Williams 3-14; Anthony Becht 1-13; Michael Clayton 1-7.

INDIVIDUAL DEFENSIVE STATISTICS

INTERCEPTIONS **SAINTS** — none.
BUCCANEERS — none.

SACKS **SAINTS** — Scott Fujita 1; Charles Grant 1.
BUCCANEERS — none.

TACKLES **SAINTS** — Josh Bullocks 10-0; Roman Harper 7-0; Scott Fujita 5-3; Scott Shanle 5-3; Jason Craft 4-0; Charles Grant 4-1; Mark Simoneau 4-4.
BUCCANEERS — Brian Kelly 8-1; Ronde Barber 6-2; Juran Bolden 4-0; Kalvin Pearson 4-1; Jermaine Phillips 4-1.

SAINTS 24 | BUCCANEERS 21

The Buccaneers' Carnell 'Cadillac' Williams, who rushed for 111 yards, finds the road to victory closed against the Saints.

STAFF PHOTO BY SCOTT THRELKELD

SAINTS 4-1 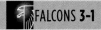FALCONS 3-1 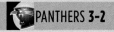PANTHERS 3-2 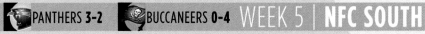BUCCANEERS 0-4 WEEK 5 | NFC SOUTH

PHILADELPHIA
Eagles

27 🔱
24 🦅

John Carney (3) celebrates with teammates Mark Campbell and holder Jamie Martin after kicking a 31-yard field goal as time expires and the Saints, who used the final 8:26, turn back the Eagles.

STAFF PHOTO BY ELIOT KAMENITZ

THE REAL DEAL

The Saints move to 5-1 with a comeback that grounds the high-flying Eagles

BY MIKE TRIPLETT Staff writer

At this point, you had to start taking the Saints seriously.

By beating the Philadelphia Eagles 27-24 at the Superdome, the Saints let the rest of the football-watching world in on a little secret. They were for real.

With a last-second 31-yard field goal by John Carney, the 14th game-winner of his career, the Saints upped their record to 5-1 and upped the ante on the rest of this remarkable season.

With another fourth-quarter comeback by their unflappable quarterback, Drew Brees, the Saints went from a nice feel-good story to the biggest bold headline of the NFL season.

With another dominant effort by the defensive line, with a turn-back-the-clock performance by receiver Joe Horn, with another 1-2 punch from tailbacks Deuce McAllister and Reggie Bush, the Saints served notice that they weren't playing around.

They were playing legitimate, bona-fide, playoff-caliber football.

"We're just playing our type of football. If you haven't seen it all year, then you haven't been watching the Saints," said cornerback Fred Thomas, who said he first recognized the confidence and expectation of success when the Saints hung on for a Week 1 victory at Cleveland.

"Now the world gets to see what we're about. We're going to have doubters all season. But we don't want anybody to give us respect, we want to earn it. And that's what we're doing right now."

The Saints earned the Eagles' respect.

They pounced early and took leads of 10-0 and 17-3, a stunning start against a Philadelphia team that also came into the game 4-1.

Then after the Eagles came back to take a 24-17 lead in the fourth quarter, the Saints responded.

They tied the score on a 48-yard touchdown pass from Brees to Horn and finished by using 8:26 on a winning field-goal drive that Bush said was "a perfect opportunity for us to go out and show our heart and show how much fight we have."

Emblematic of the effort given by the Saints, New Orleans rookie wide receiver Marques Colston refuses to go down and scores on a 7-yard pass from Drew Brees in the second quarter against Philadelphia.

STAFF PHOTO BY SCOTT THRELKELD

SAINTS 27 | EAGLES 24

That word "opportunity" came from Coach Sean Payton and from Brees, both of whom exuded a confidence that hadn't characterized this team often in the past four decades.

Brees said the message he sent to his team in the huddle in the fourth quarter, after the Saints had surrendered the lead, was that they had an opportunity to show what they're made of.

"We have confidence in what we do scheme-wise, offensively and defensively and on special teams. But I think even more so we have confidence in ourselves and each guy that plays next to the other guy," said Brees, who completed his last 11 passes after throwing two interceptions. "We have that trust and that feeling of togetherness."

The Eagles scored 21 consecutive points to start the second half, led by dangerous quarterback Donovan McNabb and young receiver Reggie Brown.

But after the Saints tied the score at 24, the Saints' defense finally stopped Philadelphia — forcing a punt after the Eagles had reached the Saints' 40-yard line.

With 8:26 remaining, the Saints took the ball and didn't give it back. They marched 72 yards and ran out the clock. The Eagles ran out of timeouts, so after McAllister ran for a first down just before the two-minute warning, Brees took a knee on three consecutive plays — setting up Carney's winning chip shot.

"Again, it wasn't pretty, but we beat a pretty good team today. I think we are a pretty good team," said Payton, who was admittedly more emotional than usual after awarding the game ball to 8-year-old Cameron Steib from Thibodaux, who was suffering from a rare muscle disease called Leigh's Disease. Steib spent time with the Saints on Saturday and Sunday as part of the New Orleans-based program A Child's Wish.

Everyone's emotions seemed ramped up after this particular victory in a season that already had several special wins.

The level of opponent had a lot to do with it, as did the dramatic finish. Payton and players did not want to say they proved anything, and they didn't want to label it a "statement game."

But they admitted that something special took place.

"I think it did," said Brees, who finished with 275 yards passing and three touchdowns.

The Saints now headed into their bye week with a one-game lead in the NFC South. They were off to their best start since 2002, when they began the sea-

TEAM	1ST	2ND	3RD	4TH	FINAL
EAGLES	0	3	14	7	24
SAINTS	10	7	0	10	27
ATTENDANCE					68,269 AT THE SUPERDOME

SCORING SUMMARY

SAINTS John Carney 39-yard field goal. Eleven plays, 47 yards in 6:04.

SAINTS Joe Horn 14-yard pass from Drew Brees (John Carney kick). Nine plays, 80 yards in 4:49.

EAGLES David Akers 47-yard field goal. Eleven plays, 51 yards in 4:49.

SAINTS Marques Colston 7-yard pass from Brees (Carney kick). Four plays, 19 yards in 1:29.

EAGLES Reggie Brown 60-yard pass from Donovan McNabb (Akers kick), 13:20. Three plays, 73 yards in 1:40.

EAGLES L.J. Smith 4-yard pass from McNabb (Akers kick). Seven plays, 76 yards in 3:51.

EAGLES Reggie Brown 15-yard run (Akers kick). One play, 15 yards in 0:06.

SAINTS Horn 48-yard pass from Brees (Carney kick). Five plays, 69 yards in 2:02.

SAINTS Carney 31-yard field goal. Sixteen plays, 72 yards in 8:26.

TEAM STATISTICS	SAINTS	EAGLES
FIRST DOWNS	22	16
RUSHES-YARDS (NET)	30-97	19-99
PASSING YARDS (NET)	275	226
PASSES (ATT-COMP-INT)	27-38-2	19-32-1
TOTAL OFFENSIVE PLAYS-YARDS	68-372	54-325
FUMBLES-LOST	1-0	2-1
PUNTS (NUMBER-AVG)	5-47.2	6-43.2
PUNT RETURNS-YARDS	3-29	2-10
KICKOFF RETURNS-YARDS	4-106	5-94
PENALTY YARDS	7-64	8-67
POSSESSION TIME	34:03	25:57
SACKED (YARDS LOST)	0-0	3-21
FIELD GOALS (ATT-MADE)	2-2	1-1

INDIVIDUAL OFFENSIVE STATISTICS

RUSHING **SAINTS** — Deuce McAllister 12-64; Reggie Bush 11-25; Aaron Stecker 3-9; Drew Brees 4-minus-1.
EAGLES — Brian Westbrook 16-72; Reggie Brown 1-15; Ryan Moats 1-7; Correll Buckhalter 1-5.

PASSING **SAINTS** — Drew Brees 27/37-3-2, 275; Joe Horn 0/1-0-0.
EAGLES — Donovan McNabb 19/32-2-1, 247.

RECEIVING **SAINTS** — Joe Horn 6-110; Marques Colston 4-40; Deuce McAllister 6-36; Reggie Bush 4-35; Nate Lawrie 1-17; Aaron Stecker 2-14.
EAGLES — Reggie Brown 6-121; L.J. Smith 4-48; Matt Schobel 2-41; Greg Lewis 1-11; Correll Buckhalter 1-10; Jason Avant 1-7.

INDIVIDUAL DEFENSIVE STATISTICS

INTERCEPTIONS **SAINTS** — Scott Fujita 1.
EAGLES — Lito Sheppard 1; Darwin Walker 1.

SACKS **SAINTS** — Hollis Thomas 1; Scott Fujita 1; Charles Grant 1.
EAGLES — none.

TACKLES **SAINTS** — Scott Shanle 6-0; Hollis Thomas 6-0; Omar Stoutmire 5-0; Scott Fujita 4-4; Fred Thomas 4-1.
Eagles — Jeremiah Trotter 8-2; Brian Dawkins 6-1; Dhani Jones 6-2; Sheldon Brown 4-2; Trent Cole 4-0.

WEEK 6 | SAINTS 27 VS. EAGLES 24 | PANTHERS 23 VS. RAVENS 21 | BUCCANEERS 14 VS. BENGALS 13 | GIANTS 27 VS. FALCONS 14

56

SAINTS 27 | EAGLES 24

Saints wide receiver Joe Horn keeps the party going after catching a 14-yard touchdown pass from Drew Brees against the Eagles in the first quarter. He finished with six catches for 110 yards and two touchdowns.

STAFF PHOTO BY SCOTT THRELKELD

SAINTS 5-1   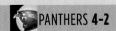PANTHERS 4-2   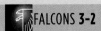FALCONS 3-2   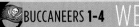BUCCANEERS 1-4   WEEK 6 | **NFC SOUTH**

BALTIMORE **Ravens**

35

22

On first-and-goal from the Ravens' 18-yard line, New Orleans tries to trip up Baltimore, having running back Reggie Bush attempt a pass to Marques Colston. But Chris McAlister (21) and Ray Lewis (52) thwart the play, with Lewis intercepting the ball in the end zone.

STAFF PHOTO BY
MICHAEL DEMOCKER

GIVING IT AWAY

New Orleans pays dearly for five turnovers and missed opportunities in a loss to Baltimore

BY JIMMY SMITH Staff writer

Even Murphy, the guy who made that whatever-could-go-wrong Law famous, probably had better days.

Ten seconds before the merciful end of a dreadful first half, Saints linebacker Scott Fujita saw Steve McNair's pass into the end zone coming directly into his waiting hands.

Suddenly, one of teammate Jason Craft's fingers altered the ball's path slightly — and Fujita watched it whiz past his reach and into the hands of Baltimore tight end Todd Heap for a touchdown, giving the Ravens a 28-7 halftime lead.

It was one of five touchdowns the Ravens scored in a thorough 35-22 thumping of the Saints at the Superdome, that in Fujita's eyes, at least, was emblematic of the nothing's-going-right theme that played itself out in front of a deflated sellout crowd of 69,152.

"It was that kind of day from the get go," Fujita said. "I didn't even get my wake-up call from the hotel. That's the kind of day it was."

As a team, the Saints (5-2) received a collective wake-up call from the Ravens (5-2) on just about every talking point Coach Sean Payton had preached all the way back to the outset of training camp in Jackson, Miss.: turnovers, plus penalties, equaled losses.

"All the things we preach about that keep you from winning games hurt us today," Payton said.

Sunday's humbling equation included five turnovers, (four interceptions, two returned for touchdowns, and one fumble), 10 penalties for 68 yards and an ankle injury to prized rookie running back Reggie Bush. He was diagnosed with a sprained left ankle.

Just as Fujita's day began inauspiciously when his hotel telephone failed to ring, the Saints' afternoon got off on the wrong foot when they failed to capitalize on an early mistake by the Ravens.

On Baltimore's second play from scrimmage, running back Jamal Lewis was hit by defensive end Will Smith, who jarred the ball loose.

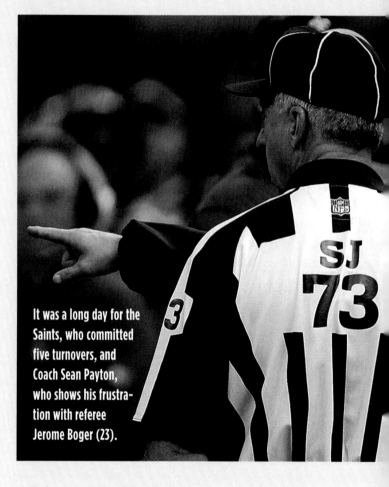

It was a long day for the Saints, who committed five turnovers, and Coach Sean Payton, who shows his frustration with referee Jerome Boger (23).

Defensive tackle Hollis Thomas fell on the ball at midfield, and 53 seconds into the game New Orleans had the chance to seize the momentum.

On the Saints' third offensive play, though, quarterback Drew Brees and Bush couldn't connect on a handoff, resulting in a fumble charged to Brees that cornerback Chris McAlister recovered at New Orleans' 43-yard line.

Eight plays later, McNair ran into the end zone untouched on a quarterback draw for a 7-0 lead.

"On third down, I'm just trying to run it to punt the ball and play the field-position game," Payton said.

Undaunted, however, the Saints came right back, thanks to a 53-yard Brees-to-Marques Colston play and a 9-yard

RAVENS 35 | SAINTS 22

STAFF PHOTO BY ELIOT KAMENITZ

Brees-to-Mike Karney pass wrapped around a 5-yard Aaron Stecker run that pushed the ball to Baltimore's 8.

On first-and-goal, the Saints were penalized 5 yards for having 12 men in the huddle, an illegal-procedure foul. On first-and-goal again, this time from the 13, tight end Nate Lawrie moved and was flagged for a false start.

On first-and-goal from the 18, Bush took a handoff from Brees and sprinted right, pulled up and lofted a pass into the end zone toward the 6-foot-4 Colston, hoping Colston could use his height advantage to win a jump ball.

Linebacker Ray Lewis, however, took the ball away from a confused Colston for the interception.

TEAM	1ST	2ND	3RD	4TH	FINAL
RAVENS	7	21	7	0	35
SAINTS	0	7	0	15	22
ATTENDANCE				69,152 AT THE SUPERDOME	

SCORING SUMMARY

RAVENS Steve McNair 5-yard run (Matt Stover kick). Eight plays, 43 yards in 4:56.

RAVENS Clarence Moore 4-yard pass from Steve McNair (Stover kick). Eleven plays, 80 yards in 6:57.

RAVENS Ronnie Prude 12-yard interception return (Stover kick).

SAINTS Joe Horn 32-yard pass from Drew Brees (John Carney kick). Four plays, 52 yards in 2:01.

RAVENS Todd Heap 6-yard pass from McNair (Stover kick). Ten plays, 71 yards in 3:58.

RAVENS Dawan Landry 12-yard interception return (Stover kick).

SAINTS Marques Colston 47-yard pass from Brees (Carney). Six plays, 74 yards in 1:19.

SAINTS Colston 25-yard pass from Brees (Brees pass to Billy Miller for two-point conversion). Six plays, 60 yards in 1:20.

TEAM STATISTICS	SAINTS	RAVENS
FIRST DOWNS	17	21
RUSHES-YARDS (NET)	14-35	39-137
PASSING YARDS (NET)	368	156
PASSES (ATT-COMP-INT)	24-46-4	17-23-0
TOTAL OFFENSIVE PLAYS-YARDS	62-403	63-293
FUMBLES-LOST	1-1	2-1
PUNTS (NUMBER-AVG)	2-44.5	6-43.2
PUNT RETURNS-YARDS	2-14	2-11
KICKOFF RETURNS-YARDS	6-136	3-50
PENALTY YARDS	10-68	9-69
POSSESSION TIME	23:14	36:46
SACKED (YARDS LOST)	2-15	1-3
FIELD GOALS (ATT-MADE)	0-0	0-0

INDIVIDUAL OFFENSIVE STATISTICS

RUSHING SAINTS — Reggie Bush 5-16; Deuce McAllister 5-11; Drew Brees 3-6. RAVENS — Jamal Lewis 31-109; Steve McNair 5-23; Musa Smith 3-5.

PASSING SAINTS — Drew Brees 24/45-3-3, 383. Reggie Bush 0/0-1, 0. RAVENS — Steve McNair 17/23-2-0, 159.

RECEIVING SAINTS — Marques Colston 6-163; Joe Horn 5-12; Mark Campbell 4-42. RAVENS — Derrick Mason 6-67; Todd Heap 3-47; Mark Clayton 1-17.

INDIVIDUAL DEFENSIVE STATISTICS

INTERCEPTIONS SAINTS — none. RAVENS — Dawan Landry 2; Ray Lewis 1; Ronnie Prude 1.

SACKS SAINTS — Hollis Thomas 1. RAVENS — Adalius Thomas 1; Trevor Pryce 1.

SAINTS 5-1 FALCONS 4-2 PANTHERS 4-3 BUCCANEERS 2-4 WEEK 7 | **NFC SOUTH**

SAINTS 5-2 FALCONS 5-2 PANTHERS 4-4 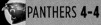BUCCANEERS 2-5 WEEK 8 | **NFC SOUTH**

#26

DEUCE McALLISTER

DULYMUS JENOD MCALLISTER

born	DECEMBER 27, 1978
birthplace	LENA, MISS.
attended	MORTON HIGH SCHOOL
	UNIVERSITY OF MISSISSIPPI
position	RUNNING BACK
height	6 FEET 1
weight	232 POUNDS
nfl experience	SIX SEASONS

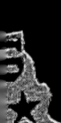

DEUCE McALLISTER

Veteran running back shows his class on and off the field

The students at Christian Brothers School gathered at the gymnasium Dec. 19, 2006, excitedly banging together their inflatable spirit sticks and cheering loudly in anticipation of Saints running back Deuce McAllister's visit.

When he arrived, they erupted into a more concise chant of "Deuce! Deuce! Deuce!"

The Saints have added an all-new collection of star power this season, but Deuce's name still rang out loudly throughout the team's fan base. McAllister, a Mississippi native and a multiple team-record holder, had earned a special place in the heart and soul of this community.

The chants of "Deeeuuuce!" were heard at Texas Stadium on Dec. 10, 2006, from an impressive showing of Saints fans during New Orleans' 42-17 victory against the Dallas Cowboys, and he received a rousing ovation from fans during the Hornets' game against the San Antonio Spurs when he appeared on the big screen Dec. 14 at the New Orleans Arena.

Teammates had shown him the same kind of respect, nominating him as this year's recipient of the Ed Block Courage Award, given to the player who best exemplified the principles of sportsmanship and courage, and the Byron Whizzer White Award, which recognized a player's work in the community.

After missing the final three months of last season with a torn anterior-cruciate knee ligament, McAllister had returned strong this season.

"He is a character guy," said first-year Saints Coach Sean Payton, who tried to reshape the Saints' roster around players like McAllister. "He is a team player, which is very important to him. He is a good worker and a talented player.

"When you start putting together a list of guys with character, toughness, intelligence and a team player, he is someone who is at the front of that list."

Through his Catch 22 Foundation, McAllister was one of the NFL's most active players in his community, in both New Orleans and his hometown outside of Jackson, Miss.

He was one of the most visible responders after Hurricane Katrina, and as a result he shared the Sporting News' Good Guy of the Year award with fellow locals Peyton Manning and Chris Duhon.

McAllister's list of community activities was lengthy, including the trip to Christian Brothers, where he accompanied fifth-grade student Scott Laiche, the winner of the JC Penney-sponsored "Take a Player to School" contest.

"I hate that you even got the media release to come," McAllister said of the school visit. "If it was left up to me, I would just go out and do it. No cameras. It's good that they get the publicity for it, but I would rather just go in, sneak in and do my deal and go out the back door.

"But it's important for me. It's just a part of me, like it is for a lot of guys on the team."

— MIKE TRIPLETT

CAREER STATISTICS

SEASON	TEAM	GAMES	STARTS	CARRIES	YARDS	AVERAGE	LONG	TD
2001	Saints	16	4	16	91	5.7	54	1
2002	Saints	15	15	325	1,388	4.3	62	13
2003	Saints	16	16	351	1,641	4.7	76	8
2004	Saints	14	14	269	1,074	4.0	71	9
2005	Saints	5	5	93	335	3.6	26	3
2006	Saints	15	13	244	1,057	4.3	57	10

POSTSEASON

SEASON	TEAM	GAMES	STARTS	CARRIES	YARDS	AVERAGE	LONG	TD
2006	SAINTS	2	2	18	161	8.9	28	1

Veteran running back Deuce McAllister missed the last three months of the 2005 season with a torn anterior-cruciate knee ligament, but in 2006, chants of DEUCE! DEUCE! DEUCE! again filled the Superdome. His blue-collar efforts drew praise, making believers out of many in the Crescent City.
STAFF PHOTO BY SUSAN POAG

Saints running back Deuce McAllister gains a full head of steam
and refuses to go down without a fight against the Buccaneers.
STAFF PHOTO BY CHRIS GRANGER

TAMPA BAY Buccaneers

31

14

PASSING GRADE

The Saints hit the halfway point of the season with momentum after dominating the Buccaneers

BY MIKE TRIPLETT Staff writer

About an hour after the Saints cruised past the halfway mark of this remarkable season, quarterback Drew Brees mentioned the word "playoffs."

It was a casual reference, which came in the context of trying to gain some momentum after the Saints' impressive 31-14 victory over the Tampa Bay Buccaneers.

But it spoke volumes about what the team had just accomplished. As in their previous victories this season, the Saints offered proof they were for real. A week earlier, the Saints (6-2) had suffered their worst loss of the season to the Baltimore Ravens, and there were just enough question marks lingering to make fans cautious in their optimism.

Those questions were answered quickly at Raymond James Stadium, where the Saints raced to a 17-0 lead, then survived a brief rally by the Buccaneers in one of New Orleans' most confident and competent performances of the season.

"We're right where we want to be," said Brees, who completed 24 of 32 passes for 314 yards and three touchdowns in perhaps his best effort to date. "We have a great challenge ahead of us. We've got some tough games on the road coming up, a tough stretch. But I think from our standpoint, we want to get on a roll. We want to get a streak going here.

"We want to just get in one of these situations where the winning continues to breed more winning, and all of a sudden you've won two in a row, three in a row, four in a row. And I think that's the kind of momentum that you can just continue to carry into December and obviously the playoffs and beyond."

Perhaps the best part of the Saints' performance was how they overcame so many missing elements.

Their momentum was gone after the loss to the Ravens, and for the first time in more than a month, the home-field advantage was gone for the Saints as well. Even more significant, the Saints made this trip without two injured starters on offense, wide receiver Joe Horn (groin) and left tackle Jammal Brown (left ankle), who remained in New Orleans.

Like a deer in headlights, Tampa Bay quarterback Bruce Gradkowski is distressed after fumbling the ball as New Orleans' Charles Grant, left, Hollis Thomas, center and Brian Young eye the prize in the first quarter.

STAFF PHOTO BY CHRIS GRANGER

SAINTS 31 | BUCCANEERS 14

Tampa Bay took more away from the Saints once the game started, when the Buccaneers' defense made a concerted effort to shut down the rushing game. Tampa Bay held New Orleans to 49 rushing yards on 35 carries.

So, the Saints adjusted and went to an aerial attack.

Rookie receiver Marques Colston continued to dazzle, with 11 catches for 123 yards and a touchdown. Third-year receiver Devery Henderson caught the two longest touchdown passes of his career, a 52-yarder in the first quarter and a 45-yarder in the third.

"One day maybe we rush for 200 yards, the next day maybe we throw for 350," Brees said. "In a perfect world, we'd like to have a nice balance where we try to keep the defense off balance. But, really, we just want to do what we do best, which is get up there with great tempo, great intensity, move the football with positive plays, convert on third downs, all those things.

"We feel like with our personnel and the tempo we play with, nobody should be able to cover everybody."

The Saints' defense was even more efficient at the start of the game, forcing Tampa Bay to go three-and-out on its first six possessions. Nearly 25 minutes into the game, the Buccaneers had gained 16 yards on their first 19 offensive plays.

Tampa Bay then broke out of its shell with two quick touchdown passes from rookie quarterback Bruce Gradkowski to Joey Galloway before halftime, a 44-yarder and a 17-yarder that narrowed the Saints' lead to 17-14.

In the second half, the Saints went back to shutting down their NFC South rivals, who fell to 2-6.

"We needed to come out and make a statement, especially after the loss we had last week," said Saints defensive tackle Brian Young, who had one of the team's four sacks. "In the past, when we started losing a game or two, you start kind of getting your head down, and you start going downhill from there. But I think this year's team is a lot more mentally strong, and there's a lot more heart on this team.

"I think it definitely shows the difference in character we have from years past."

TEAM	1ST	2ND	3RD	4TH	FINAL
SAINTS	14	3	14	0	31
BUCCANEERS	0	14	0	0	14

ATTENDANCE — 65,561 AT RAYMOND JAMES STADIUM

SCORING SUMMARY

SAINTS — **Marques Colston 15-yard pass from Drew Brees (John Carney kick).** Eight plays, 57 yards in 4:21.

SAINTS — **Devery Henderson 52-yard pass from Brees (Carney kick).** Two plays, 48 yards in 0:52.

SAINTS — **Carney 46-yard field goal. Twelve plays, 60 yards in 5:24.**

BUCS — **Joey Galloway 44-yard pass from Bruce Gradkowski (Matt Bryant kick).** Five plays, 77 yards in 2:18.

BUCS — **Galloway 17-yard pass from Gradkowski (Bryant kick).** Eleven plays, 69 yards in 1:37.

SAINTS — **Deuce McAllister 3-yard run (Carney kick). Six plays, 52 yards in 3:00.**

SAINTS — **Henderson 45-yard pass from Brees (Carney kick). Seven plays, 74 yards in 3:24.**

TEAM STATISTICS	SAINTS	BUCCANEERS
FIRST DOWNS	19	11
RUSHES-YARDS (NET)	35-49	18-68
PASSING YARDS (NET)	314	158
PASSES (ATT-COMP-INT)	24-32-0	18-31-0
TOTAL OFFENSIVE PLAYS-YARDS	67-363	53-226
FUMBLES-LOST	1-0	4-1
PUNTS (NUMBER-AVG)	6-40.3	8-40.9
PUNT RETURNS-YARDS	6-54	3-12
KICKOFF RETURNS-YARDS	3-41	4-89
PENALTY YARDS	4-25	4-25
POSSESSION TIME	37:21	22:39
SACKED (YARDS LOST)	0-0	4-27
FIELD GOALS (ATT-MADE)	1-1	0-0

INDIVIDUAL OFFENSIVE STATISTICS

RUSHING — SAINTS — Deuce McAllister 15-32; Drew Brees 6-9; Terrance Copper 1-8; Mike Karney 2-5; Reggie Bush 11-minus-5.
BUCCANEERS — Carnell Williams 12-39; Bruce Gradkowski 2-12; Earnest Graham 2-12; Michael Pittman 1-3; Michael Clayton 1-2.

PASSING — SAINTS — Drew Brees 24/32-3-0, 314.
BUCCANEERS — Bruce Gradkowski 18/31-2-0, 185.

RECEIVING — SAINTS — Marques Colston 11-123; Devery Henderson 3-111; Reggie Bush 4-22; Billy Miller 1-19; Mark Campbell 2-16; Deuce McAllister 2-12; Terrance Copper 1-11.
BUCCANEERS — Joey Galloway 4-97; Michael Clayton 4-38; Michael Pittman 6-27 0; Ike Hilliard 1-10; Alex Smith 2-8; Carnell Williams 1-5.

INDIVIDUAL DEFENSIVE STATISTICS

INTERCEPTIONS — SAINTS — none.
BUCCANEERS — none.

SACKS — SAINTS — Will Smith 2; Charles Grant 1; Brian Young 1.
BUCCANEERS — none.

TACKLES — SAINTS — Scott Shanle 8-2; Jason Craft 3-0; Scott Fujita 3-3; Charles Grant 3-2; Mike McKenzie 3-1; Will Smith 3-3.
BUCCANEERS — Derrick Brooks 9-4; Torrie Cox 9-2; Barrett Ruud 6-2; Jermaine Phillips 5-2; Shelton Quarles 5-1.

SAINTS 31 | BUCCANEERS 14

Running back Reggie Bush isn't able to break free against the Buccaneers, but New Orleans' offense had more than enough firepower as the Saints swept the season series against Tampa Bay.

STAFF PHOTO BY CHRIS GRANGER

 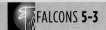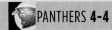

Steelers running back Willie Parker, who finished with 213 yards on 22 carries, wears down the Saints as the defending Super Bowl champions get past New Orleans.

STAFF PHOTO BY DAVID GRUNFELD

PITTSBURGH

Steelers

38 Steelers

31

IT SLIPS AWAY

Thanks to some timely thievery against New Orleans, Pittsburgh escapes with a victory

BY JIMMY SMITH Staff writer

Of all the pregame hyperbole — a guaranteed victory from Pittsburgh Steelers linebacker Joey Porter, the cutting indictment from running back Willie Parker that his teammates were complacent — it was a brief sentence from Saints quarterback Drew Brees that proved to be the most prophetic.

"It's the most telling stat in football," Brees said of the turnover margin.

Pittsburgh, a team that led the league in turnovers had none against the Saints.

And won.

The struggling defending Super Bowl champion Steelers did not turn over the ball once at Heinz Field and turned two of three Saints gifts into touchdowns in defeating New Orleans 38-31.

In the broader picture, the loss didn't seriously impact the Saints' postseason hopes, since the Atlanta Falcons didn't make up any ground in the NFC South by losing to Cleveland 17-13, and a loss to an AFC opponent didn't count in any conference tie-breaker scenarios.

That did not take the sting out of defeat, though.

"It's three versus zero," Saints Coach Sean Payton said of the miscues.

Pittsburgh entered the game at minus-11 in the take-away-giveaway category, having 10 turnovers in two previous games.

Yet it was the Saints who saw the ball slip out of their grasp three times.

First, tight end Billy Miller fumbled on New Orleans' first possession at the Saints' 32-yard line. Eight plays later, Steelers quarterback Ben Roethlisberger connected with Heath Miller on a 2-yard scoring pass to give the Pittsburgh a quick 14-0 lead.

The Steelers had driven 50 yards on the first possession for a touchdown, a 37-yard pass from Roethlisberger to Hines Ward.

But the Saints scratched back and had taken a 24-17 halftime lead and appeared to have Pittsburgh teetering

TEAM	1ST	2ND	3RD	4TH	FINAL
SAINTS	7	17	0	7	31
STEELERS	14	3	7	14	38
ATTENDANCE					61,911 AT HEINZ FIELD

SCORING SUMMARY

STEELERS	Hines Ward 37-yard pass from Ben Roethlisberger (Jeff Reed kick). Six plays, 50 yards in 3:04.
STEELERS	Heath Miller 2-yard pass from Roethlisberger (Reed kick). Eight plays, 32 yards in 4:23.
SAINTS	Terrance Copper 3-yard pass from Drew Brees (John Carney kick). Twelve plays, 52 yards in 6:06.
SAINTS	Carney 20-yard field goal. Twelve plays, 78 yards in 5:04.
SAINTS	Reggie Bush 15-yard run (Carney kick). Eight plays, 71 yards in 3:47.
STEELERS	Reed 32-yard field goal. Seven plays, 51 yards in 1:02.
SAINTS	Deuce McAllister 4-yard run (Carney kick). Five plays, 72 yards in 1:00.
STEELERS	Cedrick Wilson 38-yard pass from Roethlisberger (Reed kick). One play, 38 yards in 0:08.
STEELERS	Willie Parker 3-yard run (Reed kick). Six plays, 78 yards in 3:34.
STEELERS	Parker 4-yard run (Reed kick). Three plays, 80 yards in 0:55.
SAINTS	McAllister 4-yard run (Carney kick). Four plays, 64 yards in 1:50.

TEAM STATISTICS

TEAM STATISTICS	SAINTS	STEELERS
FIRST DOWNS	29	19
RUSHES-YARDS (NET)	29-124	26-217
PASSING YARDS (NET)	393	250
PASSES (ATT-COMP-INT)	31-47-0	17-28-0
TOTAL OFFENSIVE PLAYS-YARDS	77-517	56-467
FUMBLES-LOST	5-3	1-0
PUNTS (NUMBER-AVG)	2-39.5	3-33.0
PUNT RETURNS-YARDS	1-7	0-0
KICKOFF RETURNS-YARDS	7-158	6-135
PENALTY YARDS	3-25	5-34
POSSESSION TIME	33:01	26:59
SACKED (YARDS LOST)	1-5	2-14
FIELD GOALS (ATT-MADE)	1-2	1-2

INDIVIDUAL OFFENSIVE STATISTICS

RUSHING	SAINTS — Deuce McAllister 15-60; Reggie Bush 10-49. STEELERS — Willie Parker 22-213; Najeh Davenport 2-3.
PASSING	SAINTS — Drew Brees 31/47-1-0, 398. STEELERS — Ben Roethlisberger 17/28-3-0, 264.
RECEIVING	SAINTS — Marques Colston 10-169; Terrance Copper 6-92; Aaron Stecker 3-78. STEELERS — Hines Ward 5-86; Santonio Holmes 2-57; Cedrick Wilson 2-47.

STEELERS 38 | SAINTS 31

With time running out in the fourth quarter, wide receiver Terrance Copper hauls in a pass from Drew Brees deep in Steelers' territory, but cornerback Bryant McFadden is able to pry the ball away — with Pittsburgh recovering the ball — ending the hopes of a stirring comeback by the Saints.

STAFF PHOTO BY DAVID GRUNFELD

midway through the third quarter when linebacker Larry Foote dislodged the ball from rookie tailback Reggie Bush's grasp at New Orleans' 43, and free safety Ryan Clark recovered and returned the ball to the 38.

On the next play Roethlisberger froze cornerback Jason Craft with a play-fake and threw to wide-open Cedrick Wilson for the tying score.

Two plays after John Carney missed a 32-yard field-goal attempt wide left, Parker, who had chided his teammates in postgame comments a week ago — "This year, it seems like we already got what we want, what's the use?" he said — bounced outside of the Saints' defenders and ran 72 yards before Mike McKenzie tripped him up at New Orleans' 14. He scored from 3 yards on the first snap of the fourth quarter four plays later to put the Steelers ahead 31-24.

On Pittsburgh's next possession, Parker again went outside around the right side and raced 76 yards to the Saints' 4 before Craft chased him down. After a time-out, Parker scored on the next play to make it 38-24.

 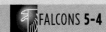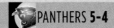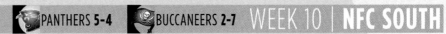

Cincinnati's Rudi Johnson, who gained 111 yards on 27 carries, finds an open space as New Orleans stumbles for the second consecutive game against an AFC Central foe.

GAME 10 | NOVEMBER 19, 2006 | SUPERDOME

CLEVELAND Bengals

31
16

STILL CHARITABLE

Miscues continue to haunt the Saints, this time aiding the Bengals

BY MIKE TRIPLETT Staff writer

The good news first. The Saints still were in contention for a playoff berth with six weeks remaining in the season.

At 6-4, they were tied for first place in the NFC South Division, and they had a chance to separate themselves from the wild-card pack if they could win at Atlanta the following week.

But here was the catch. Whatever magic had carried the Saints through the first half of this season seemed to have vanished.

More specifically, the Saints were giving it away. They turned over the ball four more times in a 31-16 loss to the Cincinnati Bengals at the Superdome.

That loss was the third in the previous four games, with a combined 12 turnovers in those three losses.

"I look at us as an offense, we're moving the ball up and down the field, scoring a lot of points, we've been great on third down, and time of possession we've been very good," quarterback Drew Brees said after throwing for 510 yards, the sixth-highest total in NFL history. "It's just that one stat. And unfortunately, the turnover stat is the most important.

"So we just go back to the drawing board, fix that, and if you have to fall back on a few others in order to fix that, so be it. Because it's the most important one."

The NFL record for passing yards in a game is held by Norm Van Brocklin, who threw for 554 yards against the Los Angeles Rams in 1951.

Brees shattered the Saints' team record of 441 passing yards in a game, set by Aaron Brooks in 2000. He also broke his personal best of 398 yards, which was set the previous week in a loss at Pittsburgh.

Against the Pittsburg Steelers, the Saints lost three fumbles. Against Cincinnati, Brees sabotaged his yardage record with three interceptions.

Two of those interceptions were back-breakers, thrown into the end zone when the Saints were inside the Bengals' 10-yard line in the second quarter. The

other was a game-breaker, returned 52 yards for a touchdown by safety Ethan Kilmer in the fourth quarter.

The Saints' other turnover was a fumble by receiver Terrance Copper during what can be described — from the Saints' perspective anyway — as an ugly second quarter.

"I think for us as an offense, we need to look at the fact that, yes, we can move the ball at will," Brees said.

WEEK 11 | BENGALS 31 VS. SAINTS 16 | PANTHERS 15 VS. RAMS 0 | BUCCANEERS 20 VS. REDSKINS 17 | RAVENS 24 VS. FALCONS 10

BENGALS 31 | SAINTS 16

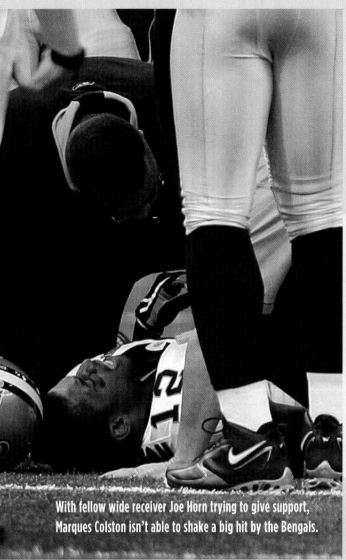

With fellow wide receiver Joe Horn trying to give support, Marques Colston isn't able to shake a big hit by the Bengals.

STAFF PHOTO BY ELIOT KAMENITZ

"Anytime, anyplace, we can move the ball. Through the air, on the ground, whatever it takes. But what it really comes down to is we have to take care of the football.

"We have to go about it in a manner that's not putting too much pressure on ourselves but saying, 'Hey, as an offense, we can be as good as we want to be as long as we just take care of this football.'"

TEAM	1ST	2ND	3RD	4TH	FINAL
BENGALS	7	3	0	21	31
SAINTS	7	0	0	9	16
ATTENDANCE					68,001 AT THE SUPERDOME

SCORING SUMMARY

BENGALS Chad Johnson 41-yard pass from Carson Palmer (Shayne Graham kick). Four plays, 67 yards in 1:52.

SAINTS Joe Horn 72-yard pass from Drew Brees (John Carney kick). One play, 67 yards in 0:11.

BENGALS Shayne Graham 21-yard field goal. Twelve plays, 76 yards in 6:25.

SAINTS Carney 24-yard field goal. Eleven plays, 74 yards in 6:33.

BENGALS Johnson 60 yard-pass from Palmer (Graham kick). Six plays, 78 yards in 3:16.

BENGALS Johnson 4-yard pass from Palmer (Graham kick). Three plays, 74 yards in 1:08.

BENGALS Ethan Kilmer 52-yard interception return (Graham kick).

SAINTS Terrance Copper 27 yard pass from Brees (Carney missed kick). Seven plays, 80 yards in 1:53.

TEAM STATISTICS	SAINTS	BENGALS
FIRST DOWNS	29	15
RUSHES-YARDS (NET)	23-91	31-119
PASSING YARDS (NET)	504	266
PASSES (ATT-COMP-INT)	37-52-3	14-22-1
TOTAL OFFENSIVE PLAYS-YARDS	77-595	54-385
FUMBLES-LOST	2-1	1-0
PUNTS (NUMBER-AVG)	5-37.2	6-41.3
PUNT RETURNS-YARDS	4-30	3-17
KICKOFF RETURNS-YARDS	5-103	3-47
PENALTY YARDS	4-25	2-10
POSSESSION TIME	33:33	26:27
SACKED (YARDS LOST)	2-6	1-9
FIELD GOALS (ATT-MADE)	1-1	1-1

INDIVIDUAL OFFENSIVE STATISTICS

RUSHING SAINTS — Reggie Bush 13-51; Deuce McAllister 10-40.
BENGALS — Rudi Johnson 27-111; Jeremi Johnson 1-6; Chad Johnson 1-3; Carson Palmer 2-minus-1.

PASSING SAINTS — Drew Brees 37/52-2-3, 510.
BENGALS — Carson Palmer 14/22-3-1, 275.

RECEIVING SAINTS — Devery Henderson 9-169; Joe Horn 3-93; Terrance Copper 6-87; Reggie Bush 8-58; Aaron Stecker 5-53; Deuce McAllister 3-29; Billy Miller 2-11; Mark Campbell 1-10.
BENGALS — Chad Johnson 6-190; Reggie Kelly 1-32; Chris Henry 2-24; T.J. Houshmandzadeh 2-15; Rudi Johnson 1-7; Chris Perry 1-5; Kenny Watson 1-2.

 SAINTS 6-4 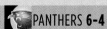 PANTHERS 6-4 FALCONS 5-5 BUCCANEERS 3-7 WEEK 11 | NFC SOUTH

79

#91

WILL SMITH

	WILL SMITH
born	AUGUST 4, 1981
birthplace	QUEENS, N.Y.
attended	PROCTOR HIGH SCHOOL
	OHIO STATE UNIVERSITY
position	DEFENSIVE END
height	6 FEET 3
weight	282 POUNDS
nfl experience	THREE SEASONS

WILL SMITH

Defensive end utilizes his leverage to bring the heat

Ask the two players who saw more of Will Smith than they'd like, teammates Jammal Brown and Jamar Nesbit, just what made Smith so good, and you got two quick answers.

"He's short," Nesbit said.

"He cheats," Brown said.

Smith, the Saints right defensive end who faced each offensive lineman in practice every day merely laughed.

"Jammal says I cheat because I know what I can get him on, and he knows what he can get me on," Smith said. "And there are a lot of short ends in the league. A bunch of guys. Size really doesn't matter."

The vertical tape measure on Smith topped out at 6 feet 3, and the scale read 282 pounds. But if you had a computer printout of Saints' defensive players ranking them best to worst, Smith's was at the top of the list.

In his third season after being drafted in the first round out of Ohio State by the Saints in 2004, Smith had become an every-down player, equally adept at stopping the run or rushing the passer, an asset to a New Orleans defense that desperately needed overall dependability.

As the left side of the Saints' offensive line, Nesbit, a guard, and Brown, a tackle, had to go against Smith in practice every day and were uniquely suited to discuss what made Smith the team's best defensive player.

"He's not the tallest guy, so he does have built-in leverage — but he's quick," Nesbit said. "And he does have speed, and at the same time, he's still strong. So the fact that he can stay on the field and play both the run and the pass, there aren't many defensive ends in the league that you don't worry about him being a liability on the run and just an asset in the pass. So that makes him special right there.

"But I think it's his leverage, and he plays bigger than he actually is. So that's always a benefit."

Said Brown: "He's got good leverage, but he's just a cheater. Gosh. No. He's a good player."

Because Smith usually was shorter than many of the linemen he went against each week, Nesbit believed that gave Smith an immediate, and at times, overwhelming advantage. And, Nesbit said, he saw it from the first day Smith was on the practice field.

"I was lucky enough to have other people go in front of me before I had to actually go against him," Nesbit said. "So I was able to see what was going on."

Smith, and was chosen to the Pro Bowl, said his position coaches at Ohio State stressed the advantage of getting underneath offensive linemen to gain the upper hand.

"I guess I was blessed, because that's what the coaches always emphasized: staying low, playing at pad level," Smith said.

— JIMMY SMITH

REGULAR SEASON

SEASON	TEAM	GAMES	TOTAL	TACKLES	ASSISTS	SACKS	INT
2004	Saints	16	40	30.0	10	7.5	0
2005	Saints	16	60	48.0	12	8.5	0
2006	Saints	14	49	31.0	18	10.5	0

POSTSEASON

SEASON	TEAM	GAMES	TOTAL	TACKLES	ASSISTS	SACKS	INT
2006	Saints	2	11	11	0	0	0

New Orleans defensive end Will Smith, who was chosen for the Pro Bowl in 2006, made some serious noise out of the gate — even as early as training camp against his teammates during practice. Yes, practice.

STAFF PHOTO BY SCOTT THRELKELD

83

Defensive tackle Hollis Thomas and the Saints get back in the win column after two consecutive setbacks, leaving quarterback Michael Vick and the Falcons scrambling to pick up the pieces.

GAME 11 | NOVEMBER 26, 2006 | GEORGIA DOME

ATLANTA Falcons

31

13

NOT VICK-TIMIZED

New Orleans sweeps Atlanta, leaps into sole possession of first place in the NFC South

BY JIMMY SMITH Staff writer

On a weekend to identify and be grateful for one's blessings, the Saints returned home thankful there was just one No. 7 on the field wearing a black jersey, gratified that there was but one dimension in which he excelled.

New Orleans came away from the Georgia Dome snapping a two-game losing streak with a turnover-free 31-13 victory over the Atlanta Falcons, and thanks to a 17-13 Washington Redskins win over the Carolina Panthers, the Saints (7-4) enjoyed a one-game lead in the NFC South with five remaining, including the regular-season finale against the second-place Panthers at the Superdome.

Yet the Saints also departed with a better understanding of what it took to be a winning, well-rounded team, thanks to the performance of Falcons quarterback Michael Vick who was, in a word, superb running the football and, in a word, ghastly throwing it.

"He's one of those amazing athletes," Saints linebacker Scott Fujita said. "He was unbelievable. I think he's faster since the last time we played him. He really kept them in the game for three quarters. I can't say enough how good that guy is. I'm almost looking forward to the film, to see a rare athlete do some of the things he did. To be on the same field with an athlete like that . . . I feel like I was in chase mode a lot today."

Yet for everything Vick did with his feet, with runs of 11, 51, 29, 15 and 38 yards among his double-digit gains, he proved the father (older Jim Mora) of his head coach (younger Jim Mora) correct in at least part of his stinging critique last week — "You need a passer at quarterback to be successful consistently in the National Football League, and he ain't getting it done in that category."

Vick didn't get it done against the Saints.

In Vick's defense, his receivers were quarterback killers, dropping a handful of passes — some of which could have been game-altering.

"I'm just doing my job by giving guys the chance to have some success," said Vick, who flipped off those of

New Orleans' Scott Fujita, left, Jason Craft, Scott Shanle and Brian Young put the hurt on Atlanta wide receiver Michael Jenkins after a 4-yard pass reception from Michael Vick in the second quarter.

STAFF PHOTO BY SCOTT THRELKELD

SAINTS 31 | FALCONS 13

the 70,933 who remained in the stands as he exited the field, "but somewhere along the line, guys are going to have to start catching the ball and making plays."

Vick's 9-of-24, 84-yard passing effort was dwarfed in comparison to the Saints' Drew Brees, who was 21-of-30 for 349 yards and two touchdowns, including a 76-yard touchdown pass to receiver Devery Henderson on the third offensive play — "Just run a deep post route, step on the cornerback's toes and get past him," Henderson said — the other a back-breaking 48-yard Hail Mary to Terrance Copper on the last play of the first half that gave the Saints a 21-6 lead.

"It was just 'go long,' " said Copper of the route that took him up the Falcons' sideline while cornerback Derrick Johnson covered him stride for stride. "I don't know if they were trying to bat it down or pick it or not. I just jumped up and tried to catch it. A great throw by Drew. It fell right in my hands."

As lopsided as the outcome was, things didn't fall right for the Saints in many ways.

Vick pummeled New Orleans' defense with his scrambles out of containment, something he didn't do in the first meeting of the season, a 23-3 Saints victory Sept. 25 at the Superdome.

But the Falcons managed just one field goal as a result of a big Vick run, a 22-yarder by Morten Andersen with 1:14 remaining in the first quarter after Vick's 51-yard gain.

After Vick's 29-yard run in the second quarter, the Saints forced Atlanta to punt.

He had a 15-yard scramble in the Falcons' second field-goal drive, a 30-yard field goal by Andersen necessitated by defensive end Will Smith's 10-yard sack of Vick on third-and-goal from the Saints' 2-yard line.

The Saints also forced a punt after Vick rushed for 38 yards in the third quarter.

"We kind of felt he was going to take over the game. It's his team. He's the leader," said Smith, who had two of the Saints' three sacks against Atlanta. "We figured any clutch situation he was going to have to step up, and we knew the ball was going to be in his hands."

Said Brees, who became the sixth quarterback in NFL history to throw for more than 300 yards in five consecutive games: "This is a great win coming off two losses. Being on the road is one thing; against a divisional opponent is another. It's like a triple whammy to come and get a win like this."

TEAM	1ST	2ND	3RD	4TH	FINAL
SAINTS	14	7	0	10	31
FALCONS	3	3	7	0	13
ATTENDANCE				70,933 AT THE GEORGIA DOME	

SCORING SUMMARY

SAINTS Devery Henderson 76-yard pass from Drew Brees (John Carney kick). Three plays, 79 yards in 1:35.

SAINTS Deuce McAllister 1-yard run (Carney kick). Seven plays, 67 yards in 3:11.

FALCONS Morten Andersen 22-yard field goal. Eight plays, 71 yards in 3:30.

FALCONS Andersen 30-yard field goal. Fourteen plays, 55 yards in 7:04.

SAINTS Terrance Copper 48-yard pass from Brees (Carney kick). Six plays, 82 yards in 1:11.

FALCONS Warrick Dunn 1-yard run (Andersen kick). Six plays, 47 yards in 2:01.

SAINTS Carney 25-yard field goal. Fourteen plays, 80 yards in 8:01.

SAINTS McAllister 9-yard run (Carney kick). Six plays, 74 yards in 1:53.

TEAM STATISTICS

TEAM STATISTICS	SAINTS	FALCONS
FIRST DOWNS	20	21
RUSHES-YARDS (NET)	25-95	45-281
PASSING YARDS (NET)	332	52
PASSES (ATT-COMP-INT)	21-30-0	9-24-0
TOTAL OFFENSIVE PLAYS-YARDS	57-427	72-333
FUMBLES-LOST	0-0	1-0
PUNTS (NUMBER-AVG)	6-44.2	6-49.2
PUNT RETURNS-YARDS	1-minus-1	2-19
KICKOFF RETURNS-YARDS	4-97	4-101
PENALTY YARDS	5-35	7-65
POSSESSION TIME	25:41	34:19
SACKED (YARDS LOST)	2-17	3-32
FIELD GOALS (ATT-MADE)	1-1	2-3

INDIVIDUAL OFFENSIVE STATISTICS

RUSHING SAINTS — Deuce McAllister 20-71; Reggie Bush 5-24. FALCONS — Michael Vick 12-166; Jerious Norwood 13-54; Warrick Dunn 19-52; Justin Griffith 1-9.

PASSING SAINTS — Drew Brees 21/30-2-0, 349. FALCONS — Michael Vick 9/24-0-0, 84.

RECEIVING SAINTS — Devery Henderson 4-158; Joe Horn 3-61; Terrance Copper 1-48; Billy Miller 3-24; Reggie Bush 3-21; Mike Karney 2-19; Mark Campbell 3-13; Deuce McAllister 2-5. FALCONS — Alge Crumpler 1-43; Roddy White 1-14; Justin Griffith 2-7; Fred McCrary 1-7; Jerious Norwood 2-7; Michael Jenkins 2-6.

INDIVIDUAL DEFENSIVE STATISTICS

INTERCEPTIONS SAINTS — none. FALCONS — none.

SACKS SAINTS — Will Smith 2; Charles Grant 1. FALCONS — Keith Brooking 1; Edgerton Hartwell 1.

TACKLES SAINTS — Jason Craft 7-0; Scott Fujita 7-0; Charles Grant 5-1; Hollis Thomas 5-1; Will Smith 4-0; Omar Stoutmire 4-1; Brian Young 4-0. FALCONS — Grady Jackson 7-0; Lawyer Milloy 7-0; Michael Boley 6-0; Keith Brooking 6-2; Allen Rossum 5-0.

Despite finding success on the ground against the Saints, Falcons quarterback Michael Vick finds Will Smith and New Orleans too much of an obstacle when it comes to the passing game.

SAINTS 31 | FALCONS 13

STAFF PHOTO BY SCOTT THRELKELD

SAINTS 7-4 PANTHERS 6-5 FALCONS 5-6 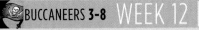BUCCANEERS 3-8 WEEK 12 | **NFC SOUTH**

SAN FRANCISCO

49ers

34

10

Saints running back Reggie Bush puts an exclamation point on his performance against the 49ers by going airborne for the final yards on a 10-yard touchdown scamper in the fourth quarter.

STAFF PHOTO BY RUSTY COSTANZA

WORTHY EFFORT

Reggie Bush's four touchdowns fuel the Saints against the 49ers as New Orleans' chances for a playoff spot improve

BY MIKE TRIPLETT Staff writer

Reggie Bush was anointed a savior when the Saints drafted him in April, he struck it rich when he signed his NFL contract in July and he nearly blew the roof off the Superdome with his first NFL touchdown in October.

But mark down Dec. 3 as the day the Saints' rookie truly arrived.

He scored four touchdowns and had 168 yards from scrimmage in a 34-10 victory over San Francisco that vaulted the Saints (8-4) ever so close to their first playoff berth in six years.

When it was over, Saints quarterback Drew Brees was asked to describe a particularly impressive play, one in which Bush made a host of would-be tacklers miss.

"He did that about eight times today, so I don't know which one you're talking about," Brees said.

This was the game fans were expecting from the 2005 Heisman Trophy winner from Southern California who was making the spectacular his specialty since before he was old enough to drive a car.

Fittingly, it was on a day when Bush's former high school coach was in the stands and his former high school quarterback, Alex Smith, was on the opposing sideline.

Bush ran the ball 10 times for 37 yards and three touchdowns, caught nine passes for 131 yards and a touchdown, and even returned one punt for 4 yards before the 49ers started aiming the ball out of bounds.

"I wouldn't say (expectations) have been too high, because nobody has higher expectations about me than myself," said Bush, who said he was more antsy than frustrated while playing more or less a supporting role in the Saints' resurgence. "It's just about staying patient through the course of the season, just waiting for my time."

It could not have come at a better time.

The Saints' eighth victory of the season was pivotal, allowing them to distance themselves from wild-card hopefuls like the 49ers (5-7).

More important, the Saints' deep and explosive

SAINTS 34 | 49ERS 10

New Orleans' Reggie Bush shows off his speed and finds the end zone for the first time against San Francisco on a 1-yard touchdown run in the second quarter.

STAFF PHOTO BY SCOTT THRELKELD

93

offense was playing a little thin against San Francisco. Their other rookie star, receiver Marques Colston, was sidelined again with an ankle injury — and Horn went down with a groin injury early in the game.

The Saints' offense was sputtering throughout the first quarter, and the 49ers' defense focused on preventing big passing plays.

Enter Bush.

Early in the second quarter, on third-and-7 from the 49ers' 15-yard line, he took a short pass from Brees, turned left and quickly found an extra gear, making three defenders grasp nothing but air. Then he fought through two more would-be tacklers and nearly reached the goal line with a convoy of blockers before landing at the 1.

Bush dived in from the 1 on the next play for his first touchdown of the game — and his third of the season.

"It was a designed play to him . . . but at some point, the athlete just takes over," Brees said of the third-down call.

Saints Coach Sean Payton said he was particularly pleased with Bush's yards after contact, something Bush was working on with running backs coach George Henshaw.

Payton praised Bush's work ethic, saying he didn't get too down on himself or put too much pressure on himself, even as more and more whispers around the league suggested that the No. 2 overall selection in the draft was "just a guy" who's not worthy of all the hype.

"I think maybe in a way we were all waiting for that breakout game," Brees said. "I'm sure the fans were all waiting for that game where he just takes the game over."

Bush scored again just before halftime, sprinting left for an 8-yard touchdown run. He scored on a 5-yard shovel pass from Brees on third-and-goal in the third quarter, and he burned three more would-be tacklers on a 10-yard sprint down the left sideline in the fourth quarter.

Bush was hardly the only hero in the Saints' most lopsided victory of the season.

Deuce McAllister pounded out a season-high 136 yards on 26 carries on the kind of day an offensive line dreams about, and cornerback Mike McKenzie ended a 25-game drought with two diving interceptions. The defense came up with three interceptions and four sacks and held the 49ers to 202 yards.

TEAM	1ST	2ND	3RD	4TH	FINAL
49ERS	**3**	**0**	**7**	**0**	**10**
SAINTS	**0**	**14**	**10**	**10**	**34**
ATTENDANCE					68,001 AT THE SUPERDOME

SCORING SUMMARY

49ERS — Joe Nedney 29-yard field goal. Thirteen plays, 64 yards in 5:58.

SAINTS — Reggie Bush 1-yard run (John Carney kick). Seven plays, 52 yards in 3:09.

SAINTS — Bush 8-yard run (Carney kick). Twelve plays, 57 yards in 5:59.

49ERS — Antonio Bryant 48-yard pass from Alex Smith (Nedney kick). Four plays, 77 yards in 2:04.

SAINTS — Carney 19-yard field goal. Four plays, 5 yards in 1:32.

SAINTS — Bush 5-yard pass from Drew Brees (Carney kick). Twelve plays, 67 yards in 6:29.

SAINTS — Bush 10-yard run (Carney kick). Six plays, 91 yards in 2:56.

SAINTS — Carney 33-yard field goal. Eleven plays, 55 yards in 7:38.

TEAM STATISTICS	SAINTS	49ERS
FIRST DOWNS	23	10
RUSHES-YARDS (NET)	41-190	15-57
PASSING YARDS (NET)	185	145
PASSES (ATT-COMP-INT)	17-28-0	14-28-3
TOTAL OFFENSIVE PLAYS-YARDS	70-375	47-202
FUMBLES-LOST	1-0	0-0
PUNTS (NUMBER-AVG)	5-42.0	7-50.3
PUNT RETURNS-YARDS	3-16	2-8
KICKOFF RETURNS-YARDS	2-71	6-137
PENALTY YARDS	3-47	7-37
POSSESSION TIME	37:19	22:41
SACKED (YARDS LOST)	1-1	3-26
FIELD GOALS (ATT-MADE)	2-2	1-1

INDIVIDUAL OFFENSIVE STATISTICS

RUSHING — SAINTS — Deuce McAllister 26-136; Reggie Bush 10-37; Drew Brees 3-14; Mike Karney 2-3.
49ERS — Frank Gore 13-40; Bryan Gilmore 1-12; Maurice Hicks 1-5.

PASSING — SAINTS — Drew Brees 17/28-1-0, 186.
49ERS — Alex Smith 14/28-1-3, 171.

RECEIVING — SAINTS — Reggie Bush 9-131; Joe Horn 1-18; Devery Henderson 2-14; Mark Campbell 2-10; Mike Karney 1-5; Jamal Jones 1-4; Deuce McAllister 1-4.
49ERS — Antonio Bryant 4-79; Arnaz Battle 4-43; Frank Gore 5-28; Vernon Davis 1-21.

INDIVIDUAL DEFENSIVE STATISTICS

INTERCEPTIONS — SAINTS — Mike McKenzie 2; Josh Bullocks 1.
49ERS — none.

SACKS — SAINTS — Charles Grant 1; Mark Simoneau 1; Hollis Thomas 1.
49ERS — Keith Lewis 1.

TACKLES — SAINTS — Charles Grant 6-0; Scott Shanle 4-3; Omar Stoutmire 4-0; Fred Thomas 3-1; Hollis Thomas 3-0.
49ERS — Keith Lewis 8-1; Mark Roman 7-1; Hannibal Navies 5-1; Marques Douglas 4-0; Walt Harris 4-2; Jeff Ulbrich 4-1.

WEEK 13 | SAINTS 34 VS. 49ERS 10 | FALCONS 24 VS. REDSKINS 14 | EAGLES 27 VS. PANTHERS 24 | STEELERS 20 VS. BUCCANEERS 3

94

SAINTS 34 | 49ERS 10

Saints cornerback Mike McKenzie rejoices in the fourth quarter after his second interception of 49ers quarterback Alex Smith as linebacker Scott Fujita (55) leads the way off the field. McKenzie hadn't caught an interception in the past 25 games.

STAFF PHOTO BY DOUG PARKER

SAINTS 8-4 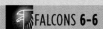FALCONS 6-6 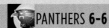PANTHERS 6-6 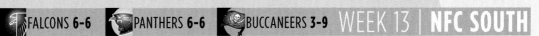BUCCANEERS 3-9 WEEK 13 | NFC SOUTH

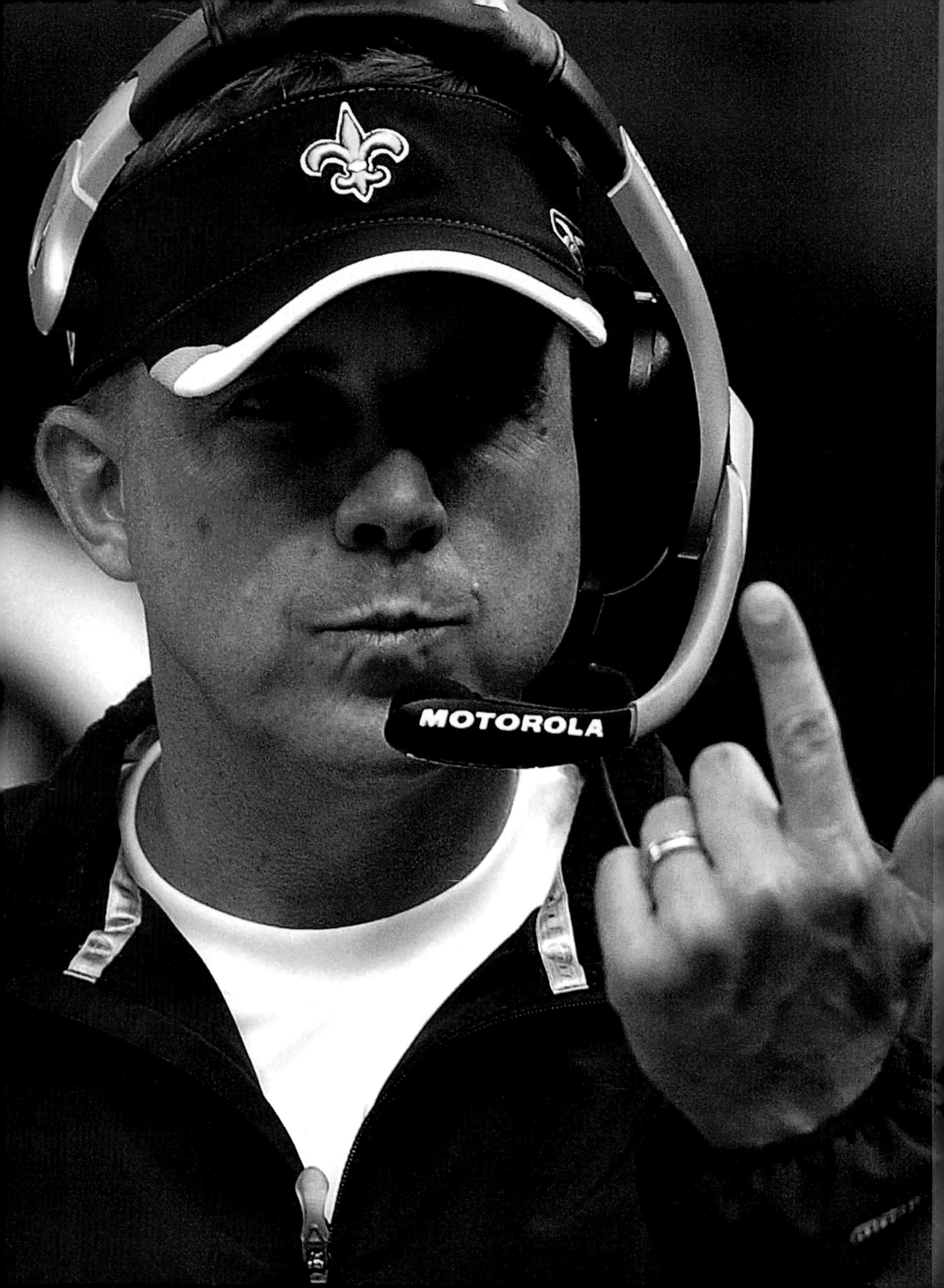
MOTOROLA

coach

SEAN PAYTON

PATRICK SEAN PAYTON

born   DECEMBER 29, 1963

birthplace   SAN MATEO, CALIF.

attended   NAPERVILLE CENTRAL HIGH

EASTERN ILLINOIS UNIVERSITY

coaching   SAN DIEGO STATE | 1988-89
experience   **on staff**

INDIANA STATE | 1990-91
on staff

SAN DIEGO STATE | 1992-93
running backs coach

MIAMI OF OHIO | 1994-95
co-offensive coordinator/quarterbacks coach

ILLINOIS | 1996
quarterbacks coach

PHILADELPHIA EAGLES | 1997-98
quarterbacks coach

NEW YORK GIANTS | 1999-2002
quarterbacks coach 1999
offensive coordinator 2000-02

DALLAS COWBOYS | 2003-05
assistant head coach/quarterbacks 2003-04
assistant head coach/passing game coordinator 2005

NEW ORLEANS SAINTS | 2006 TO PRESENT
head coach

SEAN PAYTON

First-year coach brings a new vision and instant success

Saints coach Sean Payton, who was named after a famous Roman Catholic priest, was anointed the runaway choice as NFL Coach of the Year in balloting by The Associated Press on Jan. 6, 2007.

Payton received 44 of 50 votes from a nationwide panel of sports media, capping a season in which the Saints, for 40 years an institution that had often consumed the Crescent City with an almost religious fanaticism, won the NFC South title.

Patrick Sean Payton, named 43 years ago after the Rev. Patrick Peyton, an Irish-born American priest who traveled the globe after World War II and the Korean War on what became known as "The Rosary Crusade," imploring people to pray the rosary and coining the phrase "The family that prays together stays together," had the Saints in rarefied air.

"If you research the prior winners, they all had three things in common," Payton said. "They had a great group of assistant coaches on their staff, which I feel that I do. They probably all had a great team in the locker room with players that put the team first, which in my case I do.

"And finally, they have all probably had great support from the front office and ownership. I feel that as well. I think this is something that is a reflection on many people and not just one person. I'm fortunate enough to be surrounded by a lot of good people in those areas."

Payton was the third Saints coach to win the award, joining Jim Mora in 1987 and Jim Haslett in 2000. He also was the second consecutive rookie Saints coach to earn the honor and the second to have inherited a 3-13 football team and win the distinction after capturing a division title.

Yet considering the circumstances that Payton stepped into, no past Coach of the Year winner had accomplished what Payton had in one season: Reshaping a football team that spent the previous year in a hurricane-forced exile. It only to returned to a storm-battered city and became the athletic focal point of a renaissance that arguably began Sept. 25, 2006. That day, the Saints played their first game in more than a year at the Superdome, a building that had become a national symbol of fear and destruction.

After he was hired as the 14th head coach in New Orleans history Jan. 18, 2006, Payton went about changing the way in which the city's football team was viewed and charted a course on which the Saints became a vital part of the city's recovery.

And when he met with his new football team at its minicamp after the April NFL draft, Payton spoke of the 2006 Saints' distinctive opportunity to carry out a mission no New Orleans team, no professional sports team for that matter, had ever had the privilege to undertake.

"He talked about being part of something special. Not only for the Saints, but for the city of New Orleans," Saints defensive tackle Hollis Thomas said. "And it has turned into something special."

– JIMMY SMITH

Talk about a fast start. Coach Sean Payton had fans clamoring for more after the Saints' historic run through the postseason during the 2006 season.
STAFF PHOTO BY DAVID GRUNFELD

MEET US IN THE DOME, IT'S GOIN' 5-1 DOWN!

GAME 13 | DECEMBER 10, 2006 | TEXAS STADIUM

Cowboys

DALLAS

42

17

Taking a cue from teammate Reggie Bush, New Orleans fullback Mike Karney shows that he also has the ability to stretch the defense, this time on a 3-yard touchdown pass from Drew Brees during the third quarter against Dallas. Karney, yes Karney! finished with three touchdowns against the Cowboys.

STAFF PHOTO BY SCOTT THRELKELD

STANDING TALL

The Saints show the Cowboys the ropes in a stunning road victory

BY JIMMY SMITH Staff writer

Hey, America, how 'bout them . . . Saints?

Dec. 10 was unarguably a bizarre night in Big D, where the home team was certainly unaccustomed to such thorough hide-tannings — how does New Orleans 42, Dallas 17 sound? — at Texas Stadium.

The most appealing story in the NFL this season, the resurgence of a vagabond franchise and the rebuilding of its tattered city, became even more captivating on another nationally televised stage as the Saints emphatically made their case as something a great deal more than a 2006 curiosity piece, collectively and individually.

How 'bout them Saints, genuine playoff and home-field advantage contenders and now one victory from the third division championship in their 40-year existence?

"We sent out a big message tonight," said Saints defensive end Will Smith, who had two sacks. "If you watched TV or read the paper this week, it was 'Dallas this, Dallas that.' You didn't even know who Dallas was playing. This shows we're a legitimate team."

Saints quarterback Drew Brees threw for five touchdowns (no opposing player had ever done that against the Cowboys at home) and 384 yards, making his case for MVP consideration and getting back on pace to threaten the league's single-season yardage record.

New Orleans' Sean Payton showed his mentor on the opposing sideline, Bill Parcells, that he had learned his lessons well, and likely wrapped up Coach of the Year honors.

Saints fullback Mike Karney scored his first, second and third NFL touchdowns.

New Orleans tailback Reggie Bush forcefully joined the race for Offensive Rookie of the Year with 162 yards from scrimmage, including a touchdown on a 61-yard screen pass in which he made a nifty inside cutback over the final 10 yards to the goal line.

And the embattled Saints' defense, in the strongest sense, brought Romo-mania to a screeching halt, making Dallas quarterback Tony Romo look like an undrafted free agent from a small Midwestern school.

Which he was.

Romo was 16-of-33 for 249 yards, one touchdown

New Orleans' Will Smith (91) gets the credit for sacking Dallas upstart Tony Romo, but Brian Young and Mark Simoneau (53) are more than happy to lend a helping hand as the Saints flexed their muscles.

STAFF PHOTO BY CHUCK COOK

SAINTS 42 | COWBOYS 17

SAINTS 42 | COWBOYS 17

and two interceptions, and at least two other potential interceptions were dropped, including one that bounced off Fred Thomas and into the hands of Terrell Owens for Romo's only touchdown pass.

"We did a good job of containing Tony. That was important," said Payton, who was drenched with a bucket of ice water before the end of the game by defensive end Charles Grant. "It was a good win for us."

The Saints' offense accumulated 536 total yards. No Parcells-coached Dallas team had allowed as much.

New Orleans scored on six of seven possessions from the start of the second quarter to the end of the third, the one non-scoring drive a kneel-down by Brees on the final play of the first half.

The Cowboys immediately took aim at the softened middle of the Saints' defense, absent run-stopping defensive tackle Hollis Thomas because of a four-game suspension for violation of the league's steroid policy.

On the second play of Dallas' first offensive posses-sion, running back Julius Jones took a handoff from Romo and, because of three seal blocks on the left side of the Cowboys' offensive line, burst through a huge hole and ran 77 yards untouched for a touchdown.

Undaunted, the Saints' offense, after a second failed possession, began a clock-eating, 88-yard drive starring the unsung Karney. He accounted for 31 yards on the drive, getting the score on a 2-yard plunge that tied it at 7 two plays into the second quarter.

If that wasn't enough to dampen the Cowboys' offensive enthusiasm, safety Omar Stoutmire provided his own lawn sprinkler, stepping in front of a Romo pass intended for Terry Glenn at Dallas' 39-yard line.

Capping a drive kept alive by a key Brees-to-Marques Colston 12-yard third-down pass, Karney again got the call on a pass into the left flat that he took in from 3 yards for a 14-7 lead.

Karney added a third score on a 6-yard pass from Brees in the third quarter, diving for the pylon and tap-ping the football atop it on a play that was ruled a touchdown after it was reviewed.

"This was very important; it's everything," Karney said of Payton's desire to win and his knowledge of the Cowboys' tendencies. "He knew them like a book."

The real stars on this night were the Saints, as cornerbacks Jason Craft, right, and Fred Thomas celebrate Craft's interception of the Cowboys' Tony Romo in the end zone during the third quarter.

STAFF PHOTO BY
SCOTT THRELKELD

Lessons learned

THE STUDENT, SEAN PAYTON, HUMBLES HIS FORMER TEACHER, BILL PARCELLS, IN A BIG WAY

Peter Finney

Well, folks, I've watched the Saints since they were a newly hatched expansion franchise in 1967, watched far more losers than winners, witnessed far more tears than cheers, but given the circumstances, I had never seen a better performance than the one served up by Sean Payton's football team in Cowboy country.

In prime time, the student embarrassed the professor.

In prime time, America's Team was taken apart by New Orleans' Team.

For all but a few seconds of a 60-minute war, the Dallas Cowboys were buried, left for dead, carved into little-bitty pieces, this by a relentless enemy that played smart, played tough, played with a killer instinct.

The final score, 42-17, was every bit as lopsided as the game, if not more so.

I say this because the last 10 points scored by the losers followed what looked like two cinch interceptions, one by Mike McKenzie in the end zone, another that Fred Thomas fumbled into the hands of Terrell Owens.

Yes, Saints fans, this one easily could have ended 42-7. Or more.

I was looking down during the break for the two-minute warning.

My guess was 90 percent of the Cowboy fans in a home crowd of 63,722 were on their way home.

The Saints were on the Cowboys' 9-yard-line, and Saints quarterback Drew Brees was in the process of taking four clock-eating kneel-downs, something you will seldom, if ever, see a team do against a Bill Parcells club.

I'm guessing the way it ended was somewhat difficult for the winning coach whose career owes volumes to the man he just out-coached, let's say, from Texas Stadium all the way to the Superdome.

This was a case of a rookie head coach coming up with a brilliant scheme that proved to be a mystery that a master coach could not unlock.

Payton's offensive plan, handed to a quarterback who threw for five touchdowns and 384 yards, was a piece of beauty, keeping a defense off balance, unsure,

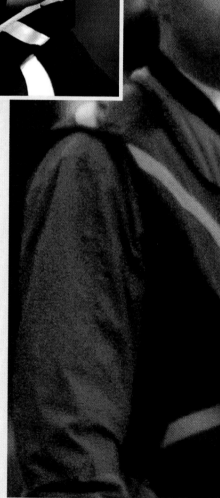

Going into the game, the edge in experience and success went to Cowboys Coach Bill Parcells, inset, over the Saints' Sean Payton. But Payton was an assistant head coach on Parcells' staff before he was hired by New Orleans, giving his insight into his mentor. By game's end, all the talk was about how Payton had schooled Parcells and how the Saints had made the leap to a playoff contender.

STAFF PHOTOS BY CHUCK COOK

SAINTS 42 | COWBOYS 17

talking to one another, the same defense that two weeks ago stymied the Indianapolis Colts and quarterback Peyton Manning.

The Saints' defensive plan did the same, to a red-hot quarterback who was 5-1 as a starter for an 8-4 club rated among the top four teams in the NFL.

It left quarterback Tony Romo confused. It rushed him into a scattershot performance by an active front, also by a secondary that locked down a quality receiving corps and came up with two interceptions.

By the fourth quarter of an evening the Cowboys had to feel would never end, America's Team had hoisted the white flag.

By then, Brees was ending his night's work by hooking up with Reggie Bush on a 61-yard scoring play, hooking up with Devery Henderson for 42 yards and six points.

The first half was a portent of things to come.

With the exception of a 77-yard Cowboys thunderbolt, the Saints played their best football of the season in the opening 30 minutes.

It was welcome to the Mike Karney Show, welcome to the Jamal Jones show, welcome back Marques Colston, welcome again to Brees.

Karney and Jones, an unlikely duo, were responsible for three touchdowns as Payton's ballclub stunned the home crowd by seizing a 21-7 lead.

It wasn't so much the score. It was how it was done. You had Brees taking the Saints 88 yards in 14 plays that consumed almost seven minutes and wound up with Karney going in from the 2 when the Cowboys were paying more attention to Bush.

Then, after an interception by Omar Stoutmire, it was Brees moving the Saints 39 yards in eight plays, this time crossing up the Cowboys once again by passing the final 3 yards to Karney.

Finally, it was a 95-yard push in nine plays, with Brees giving it life with a third-down strike to Colston, with Brees firing a 27-yard laser to Jones, coming on the play after Brees hit Jones for 22 yards but had the catch ruled a no-catch by official review.

The drive was juiced by none other Parcells, who drew a 15-yard flag by tossing a review flag inside the final two minutes — a no-no that set up the scoring toss.

If anything, for the home team, the second half was worse.

So was the final score.

On this night, the Cowboys were fortunate it ended at 42-17.

TEAM	1ST	2ND	3RD	4TH	FINAL
SAINTS	0	21	21	0	**42**
COWBOYS	7	0	10	0	**17**

ATTENDANCE   63,722 AT TEXAS STADIUM

SCORING SUMMARY

COWBOYS   Julius Jones 77-yard run (Martin Gramatica kick). Two plays, 79 yards in 0:49.

SAINTS   Mike Karney 2-yard run (John Carney kick). Fourteen plays, 88 yards in 6:44.

SAINTS   Karney 3-yard pass from Drew Brees (Carney kick). Eight plays, 39 yards in 4:04.

SAINTS   Jamal Jones 27-yard pass from Brees (Carney kick). Nine plays, 95 yards in 3:20.

COWBOYS   Gramatica 24-yard field goal. Eight plays, 66 yards in 3:34.

SAINTS   Reggie Bush 61-yard pass from Brees (Carney kick). Three plays, 74 yards in 1:27.

COWBOYS   Terrell Owens 34-yard pass from Tony Romo (Gramatica kick). Five plays, 63 yards in 2:13.

SAINTS   Karney 6-yard pass from Brees (Carney kick). Five plays, 63 yards in 2:30.

SAINTS   Devery Henderson 42-yard pass from Brees (Carney kick). Four plays, 59 yards in 1:29.

TEAM STATISTICS	SAINTS	COWBOYS
FIRST DOWNS	28	16
RUSHES-YARDS (NET)	36-159	16-116
PASSING YARDS (NET)	377	231
PASSES (ATT-COMP-INT)	26-38-0	16-33-2
TOTAL OFFENSIVE PLAYS-YARDS	75-536	51-347
FUMBLES-LOST	1-0	1-0
PUNTS (NUMBER-AVG)	4-47.8	4-40.8
PUNT RETURNS-YARDS	1-minus-2	3-21
KICKOFF RETURNS-YARDS	4-84	5-148
PENALTY YARDS	7-54	6-43
POSSESSION TIME	37:11	22:49
SACKED (YARDS LOST)	1-7	2-18
FIELD GOALS (ATT-MADE)	0-0	1-2

INDIVIDUAL OFFENSIVE STATISTICS

RUSHING   SAINTS — Deuce McAllister 21-111; Reggie Bush 6-37; Mike Karney 3-14; Devery Henderson 1-3; Drew Brees 5-minus-6.
COWBOYS — Julius Jones 10-116; Tony Romo 4-1; Marion Barber 2-1.

PASSING   SAINTS — Drew Brees 26/38-5-0, 384.
COWBOYS — Tony Romo 16/33-1-2, 249.

RECEIVING   SAINTS — Reggie Bush 6-125; Devery Henderson 2-92; Marques Colston 5-48; Mike Karney 5-39; Jamal Jones 1-27; Deuce McAllister 3-15; Mark Campbell 1-14; Billy Miller 1-12; Terrance Copper 1-8; John Owens 1-4.
COWBOYS — Terry Glenn 8-150; Terrell Owens 3-56; Jason Witten 4-33; Julius Jones 1-10.

INDIVIDUAL DEFENSIVE STATISTICS

INTERCEPTIONS   SAINTS — Jason Craft 1; Omar Stoutmire.
COWBOYS — none.

SACKS   SAINTS — Will Smith 2.
COWBOYS — DeMarcus Ware 1.

TACKLES   SAINTS — Scott Shanle 6-0; Scott Fujita 5-0; Jason Bullocks 3-1; Charles Grant 3-0; Mark Simoneau 2-0; Will Smith 2-0; Omar Stoutmire 2-0. 0.0 1 0.
COWBOYS — Terence Newman 6-1; Anthony Henry 5-0; Bradie James 5-3; DeMarcus Ware 4-0.

STAFF PHOTO BY CHUCK C

WEEK 14 | SAINTS 42 VS. COWBOYS 17   FALCONS 17 VS. BUCCANEERS 6   GIANTS 27 VS. PANTHERS 13

SAINTS 42 | COWBOYS 17

It took Saints fullback Mike Karney, center, three season to score a touchdown, but it was indeed sweet as he lets out a roar after a 2-yard plunge pulled New Orleans even with Dallas in the second quarter. Tight end John Owens, left, and running back Reggie Bush are quick to celebrate with Karney.

 SAINTS 9-4 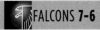 FALCONS 7-6 PANTHERS 6-7  BUCCANEERS 3-10   WEEK 14 | NFC SOUTH

Washington defensive ends and Andre Carter (99) and Phillips Daniels go high and low to lower the boom on New Orleans quarterback Drew Brees in the third quarter. Even though the Saints lost the game, New Orleans still won the NFC South title.

STAFF PHOTO BY ELIOT KAMENITZ

WASHINGTON Redskins

16

10

SWEET & SOUR

New Orleans captures the NFC South Division but loses to Washington with flat performance

BY MIKE TRIPLETT Staff writer

Perhaps the most anticlimactic moment in the Saints' 40-year history was shortly after 3 p.m., right about the time Washington Redskins quarterback Jason Campbell took a knee to run out the clock at the Superdome.

The Saints had clinched the NFC South Division, the third division title in team history and the first clinched at home.

The Redskins had triumphed 16-10.

"Yeah, we're champs, but I'm not really in the championship mood right now," Saints defensive end Will Smith said as he walked out of the "championship" locker room with his new commemorative hat and T-shirt tucked away in his travel bag.

Each player had a hat and T-shirt waiting in his locker after the game, but only a handful of players bothered to put them on.

"I won't be celebrating at all tonight, in case you're wondering," said Saints quarterback Drew Brees, who failed to throw a touchdown pass for the second time this season. "I have the shirt, and I have the hat in my bag — and I'll go home and put 'em in my closet.

"It's exciting to know that we won, but obviously the way that we won, I think we're all disappointed. Our standards are higher than maybe what you would think. We still have more that we want to accomplish."

The Saints (9-5) clinched the division because of losses by the Atlanta Falcons and Carolina Panthers. That also meant they had clinched a home playoff game, and they still were in good position to earn the NFC's No. 2 seed and a first-round bye.

New Orleans now was tied with the Dallas Cowboys (9-5) for the No. 2 seed, but the Saints held the head-to-head tiebreaker because of last week's victory at Texas Stadium.

"We shot ourselves in the foot. We could've set ourselves up really well for a first-round bye, but we're still in a great position to go and get that," said Saints linebacker Scott Fujita, who dismissed the notion that the

TEAM	1ST	2ND	3RD	4TH	FINAL
REDSKINS	**10**	**3**	**0**	**3**	**16**
SAINTS	**0**	**7**	**0**	**3**	**10**
ATTENDANCE					69,052 AT THE SUPERDOME

SCORING SUMMARY

REDSKINS Shaun Suisham 37-yard field goal. Eight plays, 52 yards in 4:34.

REDSKINS Santana Moss 31-yard pass from Jason Campbell (Suisham kick). Four plays, 80 yards in 2:01.

SAINTS Deuce McAllister 1-yard run (John Carney kick). Thirteen plays, 80 yards in 7:27.

REDSKINS Suisham 37-yard field goal. Nine plays, 60 yards in 4:04.

SAINTS Carney 41-yard field goal. Eleven plays, 56 yards in 5:16.

REDSKINS Suisham 22-yard field goal. Ten plays, 61 yards in 6:09.

TEAM STATISTICS	SAINTS	REDSKINS
FIRST DOWNS	15	19
RUSHES-YARDS (NET)	24-71	31-161
PASSING YARDS (NET)	199	193
PASSES (ATT-COMP-INT)	21-38-1	13-28-0
TOTAL OFFENSIVE PLAYS-YARDS	64-270	60-354
FUMBLES-LOST	0-0	2-0
PUNTS (NUMBER-AVG)	6-46.8	5-47.8
PUNT RETURNS-YARDS	3-20	2-26
KICKOFF RETURNS-YARDS	4-83	2-56
PENALTY YARDS	4-16	3-15
POSSESSION TIME	30:23	29:37
SACKED (YARDS LOST)	2-8	1-11
FIELD GOALS (ATT-MADE)	1-1	3-3

INDIVIDUAL OFFENSIVE STATISTICS

RUSHING SAINTS — Deuce McAllister 15-48; Reggie Bush 7-14; Mike Karney 1-6; Drew Brees 1-3.
REDSKINS — Ladell Betts 22-119; Antwaan Randle El 1-20; T.J. Duckett 4-18; Jason Campbell 4-4.

PASSING SAINTS — Drew Brees 21/38-0-1, 207.
REDSKINS — Jason Campbell 13/28-1-0, 204.

RECEIVING SAINTS — Marques Colston 7-84; Terrance Copper 3-38; Billy Miller 3-26.
REDSKINS — Chris Cooley 4-80; Ladell Betts 3-43; Santana Moss 3-37.

INDIVIDUAL DEFENSIVE STATISTICS

INTERCEPTIONS SAINTS — none. REDSKINS — Carlos Rogers 1.

SACKS SAINTS — Brian Young 1.
REDSKINS — Andre Carter 1; Marcus Washington 1.

WEEK 15 | REDSKINS 16 VS. SAINTS 10 | STEELERS 37 VS. PANTHERS 3 | COWBOYS 38 VS. FALCONS 28 | BEARS 34 VS. BUCCANEERS 31

REDSKINS 16 | SAINTS 10

New Orleans running back Deuce McAllister, who was held to 48 yards on 15 carries, is wrapped up by the Redskins' Sean Taylor (21) and Shawn Springs (24). Despite winning the NFC South, the Saints were in no mood to party.

STAFF PHOTO BY MICHAEL DEMOCKER

Saints suffered a letdown after an emotional win against the Cowboys.

Whether or not the Dallas game was to blame, the Saints were flat against the Redskins. They committed one turnover — on a fourth-quarter interception by Brees — but the offense was more sluggish than it was all year, scoring a season-low 10 points with a season-low 270 yards.

Maybe it was inevitable, like the hangover after an office Christmas party.

"I wish I had an explanation. I don't have one for you," Saints Coach Sean Payton said of a game filled with batted passes, dropped passes and great anticipation by the

Redskins' defense. "I thought we had a good week of practice, but evidently I was wrong."

The Saints' defense was adequate, allowing 161 rushing yards and forcing zero turnovers, but still holding the Redskins to 16 points.

In every other game this season, that was enough to at least force overtime and it was almost enough to win against Washington.

The Saints had one last ray of hope, getting the ball back with 4:15 remaining on their 38-yard line — but New Orleans only reached the Redskins' 15-yard line before turning the ball over on downs.

 SAINTS 9-5 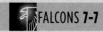 FALCONS 7-7 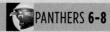 PANTHERS 6-8 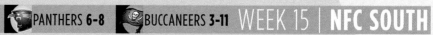 BUCCANEERS 3-11 WEEK 15 | NFC SOUTH

113

During the 2005 season, the Saints played a home game at Giants Stadium because of Hurricane Katrina and lost 27-10. During the 2006 season, New Orleans returned, with linebacker Scott Fujita, sacking Eli Manning in the third quarter, and teammates taking a giant step forward.
STAFF PHOTO BY MICHAEL DEMOCKER

New York Giants

30

7

BYE, BYE

The Saints rout the Giants despite the efforts of Tiki Barber and get a week off in the postseason

BY JIMMY SMITH Staff writer

In a week, in nearby Times Square, revelers rang out the old and ushered in the new.

A figurative ball drop came seven days earlier at Giants Stadium as 78,539 fans witnessed a similar athletic transition.

The veteran running back, who credited Saints Coach Sean Payton for making him a possible Hall of Fame candidate, went out in a bittersweet celebration; a new one, whose similar talents were refined and exploited this season by Payton, became the same type of well-rounded offensive threat by reaching the 100-yard rushing plateau for the first time in the 15th game of his rookie season.

The Saints, meanwhile, took care of their end of the first-round bye equation with a dominating 30-7 victory over the New York Giants, who bade farewell to Tiki Barber and vainly attempted to tackle Reggie Bush, who finished with 126 yards and a touchdown on 20 carries. Backfield mate Deuce McAllister had 108 yards on 27 carries.

The Saints (10-5) awaited the outcome of Monday's Dallas Cowboys-Philadelphia Eagles game to determine if the NFC South champions would enter the postseason as the No. 2 seed with a first-round bye.

Dallas lost, securing a week off for the Saints.

Bush, who left the stadium without formally speaking with reporters, saying he had to meet his family, said he spoke with Barber during pregame warmups, and the old and the young traded pleasantries.

"Before the game I told him, 'I hate seeing you retire; I wish you wouldn't retire,'" Bush said of the conversation. "He said he had to make room for young guys like me."

Barber, who was transformed from a seldom-used third-down back when Payton first arrived with the Giants as an assistant coach in 1999 but became a versatile every-down threat at Payton's urging, finished with 71 yards on 16 carries. He caught three passes for 12 yards.

The Saints' defense saw to it that Barber's last game at the Meadowlands wasn't one he would necessarily

STAFF PHOTO BY MICHAEL DEMOCKER

116

SAINTS 30 | GIANTS 7

New Orleans' 1-2 attack of Deuce McAllister, eluding a host of Giants, and Reggie Bush was running on all cylinders. McAllister had 27 carries for 108 yards, and Bush finished with 126 yards on 20 carries.

remember.

"It wasn't a good product today," Barber said. "It was an embarrassing product."

New York's offense managed 142 yards on 45 offensive snaps. Quarterback Eli Manning was 9-of-25 with an interception but was victimized by several dropped passes by his receiving corps. The Giants (7-8) did not convert any third-down attempts in 10 tries and failed on their only fourth-down try.

New York did not have a snap in Saints' territory the entire game — the Giants' score came on a 55-yard touchdown pass from Manning to Plaxico Burress in the first quarter when cornerback Fred Thomas stumbled at the line of scrimmage, leaving Burress wide open.

The Saints had a 2-to-1 advantage in time of possession, holding the ball for 40 minutes, 34 seconds to the Giants' 19:26, including a clock-gobbling 18-play, 89-yard drive in the second quarter that consumed 8:39, one in which Bush accounted for 70 of the march's total yardage.

"I thought we played outstanding on defense," Payton said. "The guys did a good job staying focused on the task at hand. Our defense was magnificent."

The Giants' defense, bolstered by the return of defensive end Michael Strahan, the NFL's all-time career sacks leader, got to Saints quarterback Drew Brees once, dropping him for a 9-yard loss.

Strahan, who was blocked by right tackle Jon Stinchcomb, had just five tackles and knocked down one pass. Giants right defensive end Osi Umenyiora had the only sack and six tackles.

Giants Coach Tom Coughlin said his team came in expecting to win, certain it would send Barber, the only New York player announced in pregame introductions and the subject of a JumboTron halftime tribute, out as a winner.

"I would have liked that to have been (a win) for Tiki's last game here at home, and I think all of the players felt the same way," Coughlin said.

Payton, who embraced Barber at midfield at game's end and expressed to Barber his admiration, had other thoughts.

"The special part of today, is a real good running back, a Hall of Fame running back, finished up his career here," Payton said. "He's a special person as well as a player. I know this town, and this league will miss him."

TEAM	1ST	2ND	3RD	4TH	FINAL
SAINTS	3	10	7	10	30
GIANTS	7	0	0	0	7

ATTENDANCE — 78,539 AT GIANTS STADIUM

SCORING SUMMARY

GIANTS — Plaxico Burress 55-yard pass from Eli Manning (Jay Feely kick). Four plays, 67 yards in 2:17.

SAINTS — John Carney 32-yard field goal. Four plays, 4 yards in 1:25.

SAINTS — Carney 26-yard field goal. Twelve plays, 55 yards in 3:27.

SAINTS — Marques Colston, 2-yard pass from Drew Brees (Carney kick). Eighteen plays, 89 yards in 8:39.

SAINTS — Reggie Bush 1-yard run (Carney kick). Five plays, 51 yards in 2:19.

SAINTS — Deuce McAllister 9-yard run (Carney kick). Ten plays, 62 yards in 5:22.

SAINTS — Carney 38-yard field goal. Four plays, 4 yards in 1:34.

TEAM STATISTICS

TEAM STATISTICS	SAINTS	GIANTS
FIRST DOWNS	22	6
RUSHES-YARDS (NET)	53-236	18-83
PASSING YARDS (NET)	123	59
PASSES (ATT-COMP-INT)	12-32-0	9-25-1
TOTAL OFFENSIVE PLAYS-YARDS	86-359	45-142
FUMBLES-LOST	0-0	2-2
PUNTS (NUMBER-AVG)	5-42.6	9-37.6
PUNT RETURNS-YARDS	5-15	2-8
KICKOFF RETURNS-YARDS	2-62	7-164
PENALTY YARDS	2-15	7-67
POSSESSION TIME	40:34	19:26
SACKED (YARDS LOST)	1-9	2-15
FIELD GOALS (ATT-MADE)	3-4	0-0

INDIVIDUAL OFFENSIVE STATISTICS

RUSHING — SAINTS — Reggie Bush 20-126; Deuce McAllister 27-108; Mike Karney 1-3; Drew Brees 5-minus-1.
GIANTS — Tiki Barber 16-71; Jim Finn 1-12; Eli Manning 1-0; Shaun O'Hara 1-0.

PASSING — SAINTS — Drew Brees 13/32-1-0, 132.
GIANTS — Eli Manning 9/25-1-1, 74.

RECEIVING — SAINTS — Terrance Copper 2-46; Marques Colston 4-37; Reggie Bush 2-23; Deuce McAllister 2-14; Mark Campbell 1-8; Aaron Stecker 2-4.
GIANTS — Plaxico Burress 1-55; Tiki Barber 3-12; Tim Carter 1-9; Jim Finn 1-1; Sinorice Moss 1-0; Jeremy Shockey 2-minus-3.

INDIVIDUAL DEFENSIVE STATISTICS

INTERCEPTIONS — SAINTS — Fred Thomas 1.
GIANTS — none.

SACKS — SAINTS — Scott Fujita 1; Scott Shanle 1.
GIANTS — Osi Umenyiora 1.

TACKLES — SAINTS — Jay Bellamy 4-1; Charles Grant 4-2; Fred Thomas 4-0; Josh Bullocks 3-1; Jason Craft 3-0; Scott Fujita 3-2; Scott Shanle 3-0.
GIANTS — Will Demps 10-1; Antonio Pierce 8-4; R.W. McQuarters 6-1; Brandon Short 6-4; Osi Umenyiora 5-1.

SAINTS 30 | GIANTS 7

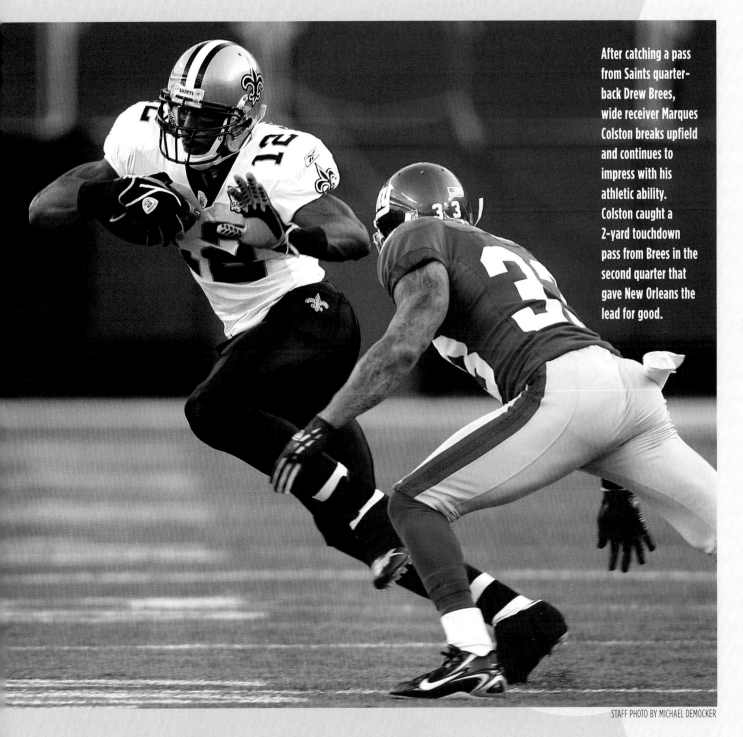

After catching a pass from Saints quarterback Drew Brees, wide receiver Marques Colston breaks upfield and continues to impress with his athletic ability. Colston caught a 2-yard touchdown pass from Brees in the second quarter that gave New Orleans the lead for good.

STAFF PHOTO BY MICHAEL DEMOCKER

 SAINTS **10-5** FALCONS **7-8**  PANTHERS **7-8** 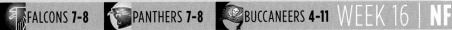 BUCCANEERS **4-11** WEEK 16 | **NFC SOUTH**

Having secured a first-round bye in the playoffs, New Orleans rested most of its starters against Carolina. Panthers wide receiver Steve Smith found the going easier, including a 15-yard touchdown pass from Jake Delhomme against safety Bryan Scott in the third quarter.

CAROLINA Panthers

31

21

SAFETY TACTICS

Playoff-bound New Orleans rest its starters in a losing effort to Carolina

BY MIKE TRIPLETT Staff writer

Happy new year, Saints fans.

Any chance 2007 can top 2006?

Sure, this past year ended on a bit of a whimper, with the Saints resting most of their starters during an inconsequential 31-21 loss to the Carolina Panthers.

But it was the 364 days leading up that made 2006 the most spectacular year in Saints history.

Now, for an encore, they had two weeks to prepare for the playoff opener at the Superdome, when they hosted a second-round playoff game for the first time against the Philadelphia Eagles.

"We've already beaten a lot of odds. We might as well just keep beating them," said Saints quarterback Drew Brees, who had a short but sweet performance in Sunday's regular-season finale, leading the Saints on a touchdown drive before leaving to raucous cheers.

His day was supposed to be even shorter. Because the Saints (10-6) had clinched a first-round bye for the first time in team history, the plan was for Brees to leave Sunday after two plays.

But Brees fumbled the second snap of the game — that teammate Reggie Bush recovered — and Brees and Coach Sean Payton agreed that it wasn't fitting for Brees to go out like that.

The next play was a 6-yard pass to Bush, then a 25-yard pass from Brees to tight end John Owens.

"Then it's like, 'OK, now we're deep in their territory. You can't pull me out now. We have to score,'" Brees said, explaining that all of this was conveyed through nonverbal glances between him and Payton across the field. "It wasn't until after we got in the end zone, then he said, 'All right, you're running one more play. It's going to be a run play, and then you're out.'"

Brees handed off the ball one last time, then the Saints called timeout so he was able to run off the field to a proper sendoff from the second-largest reported crowd of the season.

"It was neat," Brees said. "During that time I was

With Sean Payton playing his starters sparingly against Carolina, quarterback Drew Brees, who played one series, finds the time to give his coach a pat on the back.

STAFF PHOTO BY RUSTY COSTANZA

coming off the field, it gave me a chance to reflect on how far we have come this season.

"I think about that and what it means to this city. When you think back to six months ago, who would have ever thought that we would be sitting here with a first-round bye and are about to play a home playoff game. It has been a team effort, a city effort, a fan effort.

"That was an opportunity for me to think, 'Wow, we have some of the best fans in the world.'"

That first touchdown was a 1-yard run by Bush, which

PANTHERS 31 | SAINTS 21

TEAM	1ST	2ND	3RD	4TH	FINAL
PANTHERS	**7**	**7**	**14**	**3**	**31**
SAINTS	**7**	**7**	**7**	**0**	**21**
ATTENDANCE					69,569 AT THE SUPERDOME

SCORING SUMMARY

SAINTS — Reggie Bush 1-yard run (John Carney kick). Eight plays, 65 yards in 3:51.

PANTHERS — Steve Smith 22-yard pass from Jake Delhomme (John Kasay kick). Nine plays, 73 yards in 5:53.

SAINTS — Jamaal Branch 8-yard pass from Jamie Martin (Carney kick). Three plays, 73 yards in 1:38.

PANTHERS — DeShaun Foster 2-yard run (Kasay kick). Fourteen plays, 85 yards in 7:36.

PANTHERS — Chris Gamble 18-yard interception return (Kasay kick).

PANTHERS — Smith 15-yard pass from Delhomme (Kasay kick). Two plays, 24 yards in 0:50.

SAINTS — Fred McAfee 6-yard run (Carney kick). Eleven plays, 78 yards in 4:52.

PANTHERS — Kasay 19-yard field goal. Nine plays, 64 yards in 5:07.

TEAM STATISTICS

TEAM STATISTICS	SAINTS	PANTHERS
FIRST DOWNS	13	20
RUSHES-YARDS (NET)	17-61	33-106
PASSING YARDS (NET)	236	207
PASSES (ATT-COMP-INT)	20-29-1	23-27-0
TOTAL OFFENSIVE PLAYS-YARDS	51-297	60-313
FUMBLES-LOST	4-1	0-0
PUNTS (NUMBER-AVG)	5-44.8	5-49.8
PUNT RETURNS-YARDS	4-13	2-11
KICKOFF RETURNS-YARDS	5-153	4-84
PENALTY YARDS	4-38	2-19
POSSESSION TIME	25:21	34:39
SACKED (YARDS LOST)	5-18	0-0
FIELD GOALS (ATT-MADE)	0-0	1-1

INDIVIDUAL OFFENSIVE STATISTICS

RUSHING — SAINTS — Jamaal Branch 10-29; Reggie Bush 3-20; Fred McAfee 3-2; Drew Brees 1-0.
PANTHERS — DeShaun Foster 19-79; Steve Smith 1-21; DeAngelo Williams 9-7; Brad Hoover 1-2; Jack Delhomme 3-minus-3.

PASSING — SAINTS — Jamie Martin 16/24-1-1, 208; Drew Brees 4/5-0-0, 46.
PANTHERS — Jake Delhomme 23/27-2-0, 207.

RECEIVING — SAINTS — Devery Henderson 2-71; Jamal Jones 3-69; John Owens 3-40; Billy Miller 3-33; Jamaal Branch 5-14; Mike Karney 2-14; Reggie Bush 2-13.
PANTHERS — Steve Smith 7-85; DeAngelo Williams 6-52; Keyshawn Johnson 3-24; Brad Hoover 3-22; DeShaun Foster 3-12; Michael Gaines 1-12.

gave the Saints a quick 7-0 lead and thrilled the home fans — especially when Bush leaped about 9 feet into the stands to celebrate.

The Saints' other two touchdowns were even more special: a 7-yard reception by rookie Jamaal Branch in the first game of his career, and a 6-yard run by Fred McAfee in his 194th game.

But that wasn't enough to beat the Panthers on a day when Carolina's first string beat up on New Orleans' second- and third-stringers.

SAINTS 10-6   PANTHERS 8-8   FALCONS 7-9   BUCCANEERS 4-12   WEEK 17 | NFC SOUTH

With the Superdome rocking just like it had for a 'Monday Night Football' game against the Falcons on Sept. 25, 2006, the Saints again entered the field with a sense of urgency. This time the matchup was against the Eagles in an NFC divisional playoff game. At stake: a spot in the NFC championship game. New Orleans didn't disappoint.

STAFF PHOTO BY MICHAEL DEMOCKER

NFC DIVISIONAL PLAYOFF

JANUARY 13, 2007 | SUPERDOME

PHILADELPHIA Eagles

27

24

HISTORIC STEP

Deuce McAllister runs wild as New Orleans edges Philadelphia to advance to the NFC championship game

BY JIMMY SMITH Staff writer

Hey, New Orleans, felt that rush of cold air under your feet?

Yeah, hell was beginning to freeze over.

The Saints, for 10 years less than half a century the butt of that long-standing joke about when they might win a title, found themselves one victory away from the NFC championship and a trip to Super Bowl XLI in Miami, thanks to a 27-24 victory over the Philadelphia Eagles in a divisional playoff game at a delirious Superdome.

Deuce McAllister's 5-yard, third-down run with 1:37 remaining, with the Eagles' having exhausted their timeouts, set up two kneel-downs by quarterback Drew Brees that ran out the clock but extended the season another week.

Seconds after McAllister's game-clinching run — his 11-yard catch-and-run on a Brees' screen pass with 1:05 remaining in the third quarter provided the winning points — Coach Sean Payton thrust his arm skyward, setting off a raucous celebration by the 70,001 in attendance and, no doubt, hundreds of thousands of Saints fans throughout the region weary of daily struggles for existence in a post-storm city and 40 years of heartbreak from its star-crossed football team.

"We've got high goals," Payton said. "And I couldn't be happier for the people in this town who've been through so much. Our fans here are fantastic. They were a big part of this win tonight, a big part of it all season. It's an exciting win for us, and it's another challenge next weekend."

The final score matched the count by which the Saints defeated the Eagles in the regular season Oct. 15 at the Superdome.

But this time, it followed a different script.

In the first meeting, the Saints used an 8-minute, 26-second drive at the end of the game, driving to a 31-yard John Carney field goal on the last play for the victory.

This time, the Saints had to overcome big plays by the Eagles' offense — a 75-yard Jeff Garcia-to-Donté Stallworth touchdown pass and a 62-yard touchdown

STAFF PHOTO BY CHUCK COOK

SAINTS 27 | EAGLES 24

Out of the gate, the Saints relied on running back Deuce McAllister to set the tone on offense against the Eagles in a physical matchup.

New Orleans running back Deuce McAllister, having had his helmet knocked off, isn't denied as he scores on a 5-yard run — with a big push from his teammates — in the third quarter against Philadelphia. Wide receiver Terrance Copper (18) signals the touchdown.

STAFF PHOTO BY SCOTT THRELKELD

run by Brian Westbrook — and a bad-pitch turnover by Brees on a running play for Reggie Bush with 3:18 remaining at Philadelphia's 44-yard line that put the pressure on New Orleans' defense to keep the Eagles out of David Akers' field-goal range.

Two big plays by linebacker Scott Fujita, first on a tackle of Westbrook on second-and-11 for a 1-yard gain, the second a furious up-the-middle rush on Garcia on third down that forced an incompletion.

A crowd-induced false-start penalty on fourth-and-10 from the 44-yard line forced the Eagles to punt, and the Saints, with McAllister, who gained 143 yards on 21 carries with a rushing touchdown, doing the ground work to accomplish that vital first down.

"Obviously, it's an exciting win for this team, this organization, and this city," Payton said. "I couldn't be more proud of a group of guys who've fought and battled. But take your hats off to the Eagles and (Coach) Andy Reid. His team came in here, and his team has done something else these last six weeks (all wins). That's a good team we beat tonight, and it came right down to the wire."

Agonizingly so.

The Saints squandered their first chance to put the game away, getting the ball with eight minutes remaining, leading 27-24 after the defense had held the Eagles to a 24-yard Akers field goal earlier in the quarter.

On the strength of McAllister's legs, the Saints had driven to the Eagles' 32 when Brees' pitch wasn't grasped by Bush.

Former Saints defensive end Darren Howard fell on the loose ball at the Eagles' 44.

The Saints' defense, perceived to be a weak spot this season, stopped the Eagles when it mattered most.

It wasn't that way early on, though.

Garcia continued doing what he had done throughout Philadelphia's six-game winning streak that brought the Eagles to that point. He was mistake-free in the first half, though the Saints' secondary had its hands on four passes in the first quarter alone, three of which free safety Josh Bullocks could not gather in.

In the second quarter, Garcia didn't put the ball anywhere near Saints' defensive backs.

Instead, Garcia found wide-open receivers with New Orleans defenders seeing nothing but the numbers on the Eagles' backs. First off it was Stallworth, who gathered in a Garcia rainbow at the Saints' 20 and took it in the rest of the way untouched for a 75-yard touchdown.

That erased a 6-0 New Orleans lead and, for a

DEUCE! DEUCE! DEUCE!
Saints quarterback Drew Brees congratulates Deuce McAllister after McAllister caught an 11-yard touchdown pass from Brees in the third quarter. McAllister rushed for 143 yards on 21 carries, and he caught four passes for 20 yards.

STAFF PHOTO BY MICHAEL DEMOCKER

moment, seemed to suck the air from the building.

New Orleans came right back, though, with a 14-play, 78-yard drive that ran 8:19 off the clock, Payton and Brees using a balanced mix of runs by McAllister and passes to Bush and Marques Colston.

Bush gave the Saints the lead again on a 4-yard run with 5:19 remaining in the first half, getting jammed in the middle of the line, then bouncing out to the right in a race for the end zone pylon.

He won.

Garcia, though, showed his and the Eagles' resilien-

cy. He completed a 32-yard third-down pass to Reggie Brown, then had a 25-yard third-down completion to Hank Baskett. Westbrook leaped over from a yard out for a touchdown with 50 seconds remaining in the half for a 14-13 lead at the break.

The Saints nearly had their second successful half-ending Hail Mary pass, but Philadelphia's William James stripped the ball from a falling Colston in the end zone.

The play was not reviewed by replay officials in the booth. That would have made the second half a little less stressful, but what's a little stress when 40 years of suffering was about to be relieved?

"The fans who've followed this team have been through a lot," Payton said. "More thin than thick. They've been loyal and passionate. They come from everywhere. It's gratifying to win, to get them fired up about their team. Everything that has gone on here, within the last year and a half, Katrina, and how much recover we still have to go, New Orleans still has to go, this is a bright spot.

"This is a different team, a different time."

When needed most

NEW ORLEANS' DEFENSE RISES TO THE OCCASION

John DeShazier

It caused your heart to skip while showing its own, this Saints defense.

It allowed enough big plays to make a priest cuss and a non-drinker swig like a corner wino. It appeared lost often enough to cause the gray to override today's dye job. It gave so much ground that it found itself with no wall to have its back against.

But it came through when it had to. And against the Eagles, it had to more than it ever had this season, had to because if it didn't the dream season was dead right there on the Superdome turf, had to because the Coach of the Year in the NFL was a little too cute a little too often and needed someone — anyone — to throw a knockout punch.

And the defense that was chewed up by Philadelphia like a stick of gum in a nervous mouth supplied it.

Two fourth-quarter defensive stops, and the Saints ended the Eagles' season. Two fourth-quarter defensive stands, and New Orleans kept alive its hopes to stand atop NFL's mountain.

Two bare-knuckled rounds, and the Saints walked out of the ring with a 27-24 victory in their NFC divisional playoff game and into franchise history. Now, for the first time, the team played for the NFC title.

"We're a team; things happen," said defensive end Charles Grant, who wreaked havoc against the Eagles. "As a football team, we were able to stand up for what we believe in. All 11 guys on defense were able to stand up."

Said New Orleans Coach Sean Payton: "We've got to make some corrections. We've got to play better."

True, but what counted was that they played well enough against the Eagles.

Granted, the recipe wasn't all that attractive.

Generally, when a team allows 240 yards passing and a touchdown (to Jeff Garcia) and 113 yards rushing and two touchdowns (to Brian Westbrook), the result wasn't going to be pretty.

But the two stops, after the Eagles closed to 27-24, were majestic in their result, brutal in their efficiency. And, actually, the stop count was raised to three if we add in Philadelphia's last score, because that field goal was forced after the Eagles drove to second-and-goal

from the Saints' 4-yard line.

The first snuff took place with 9:24 remaining, with the Eagles going three-and-out after having a first down at their 37, not gaining a yard courtesy of two incomplete passes and one tackle for no gain on Westbrook. The next happened after a Saints fumble, with the Eagles taking possession at their 44 with 3:18 remaining. Philadelphia didn't gain a yard in three plays, went for it on fourth down, took a 5-yard penalty for a false start — then punted on fourth-and-15.

Every ounce of the effort was needed, in part because the offense was a little shaky even while rolling up more than 400 yards and 27 points.

First, Deuce McAllister was a tad underworked. His 21 carries for 143 yards could have been 10 carries and 50 yards more if he was fed as much as he should have been against the Eagles, who had no answer to his bruising runs. The Eagles looked as if they wanted no part of McAllister, who in the third quarter bulled his way in from 5 yards with a little help from his friends and scored on an 11-yard pass from Drew Brees.

Second, that misdirection pitch from Brees to Reggie Bush on the next-to-last offensive possession was, in a word, "loose." A little too loose for a team that was hanging on by its fingernails and would've come out better — and safer — taking a knee than doing anything that required the flight of the football.

"The defense came out with field position (against them)," Payton said. "They bowed up and got a three-and-out."

And turned over the game to McAllister, who ran for 4, 5 and 5 yards on the next three offensive plays to close out the game.

"He just had that look in his eye," Brees said of McAllister. "He's a horse. When we needed the big runs. He delivered."

And when they needed to stop Philadelphia's run, the Saints' defense delivered.

Twice.

"When plays have to be made, guys step up and make them," New Orleans linebacker Scott Fujita said.

Now that they had stepped up, they had walked into the NFC title game.

SAINTS 27 | EAGLES 24

With their season hanging in the balance, New Orleans' Will Smith (91) and Hollis Thomas corral Philadelphia running back Correll Buckhalter. The Saints' hung on against the Eagles, thanks in large part to a goal-line stand — only giving up a field goal — in the fourth quarter and another defensive stop with less than two-minutes remaining.

STAFF PHOTO BY SCOTT THRELKELD

TEAM	1ST	2ND	3RD	4TH	FINAL
EAGLES	0	14	7	3	24
SAINTS	3	10	14	0	27

ATTENDANCE 70,001 AT THE SUPERDOME

SCORING SUMMARY

SAINTS John Carney 33-yard field goal. Five plays, 35 yards in 2:05.

SAINTS Carney 23-yard field goal. Six plays, 59 yards in 1:33.

EAGLES Donté Stallworth 75-yard pass from Jeff Garcia. (David Akers kick). Three plays, 76 yards in 1:08.

SAINTS Reggie Bush 4-yard run (Carney kick). Fourteen plays, 78 yards in 8:19.

EAGLES Brian Westbrook 1-yard run (Akers kick). Eleven plays, 80 yards in 4:29.

EAGLES Westbrook 62-yard run (Akers kick). Three plays, 80 yards in 1:35.

SAINTS Deuce McAllister 5-yard run (Carney kick). Seven plays, 63 yards in 3:49.

SAINTS McAllister 11-yard pass from Drew Brees (Carney kick). Nine plays, 84 yards in 6:21.

EAGLES Akers 24-yard field goal. Nine plays, 64 yards in 11:08.

TEAM STATISTICS

TEAM STATISTICS	SAINTS	EAGLES
FIRST DOWNS	27	14
RUSHES-YARDS (NET)	37-208	20-123
PASSING YARDS (NET)	227	232
PASSES (ATT-COMP-INT)	20-32-0	15-30-0
TOTAL OFFENSIVE PLAYS-YARDS	72-435	51-355
FUMBLES-LOST	2-1	1-0
PUNTS (NUMBER-AVG)	3-40.3	6-38.5
PUNT RETURNS-YARDS	3-21	2-13
KICKOFF RETURNS-YARDS	5-137	4-112
PENALTY YARDS	3-35	6-39
POSSESSION TIME	35:24	24:36
SACKED (YARDS LOST)	3-16	1-8
FIELD GOALS (ATT-MADE)	2-2	1-1

INDIVIDUAL OFFENSIVE STATISTICS

RUSHING **SAINTS** — Deuce McAllister 21-143; Reggie Bush 12-52; Steve Weatherford 1-15; Drew Brees 3-minus-2.
EAGLES — Brian Westbrook 13-116; Jeff Garcia 4-9; Correll Buckhalter 3-minus-2.

PASSING **SAINTS** — Drew Brees 20/32-1-0, 243.
EAGLES — Jeff Garcia 15/30-1-0, 240.

RECEIVING **SAINTS** — Billy Miller 4-64; Marques Colston 5-55; Devery Henderson 1-35; Mark Campbell 1-23; Reggie Bush 3-22; John Owens 1-21; Deuce McAllister 4-20; Terrance Copper 1-3.
EAGLES — Donté Stallworth 3-100; Reggie Brown 3-76; Hank Baskett 1-25; L.J. Smith 2-23; Correll Buckhalter 1-8; Matt Schobel 1-5; Brian Westbrook 3-5; Thomas Tapeh 1-minus-2.

INDIVIDUAL DEFENSIVE STATISTICS

INTERCEPTIONS **SAINTS** — none. **EAGLES** — none.

SACKS **SAINTS** — Scott Shanle 1.
EAGLES — Darwin Walker 1; Trent Cole 1.

TACKLES **SAINTS** — Will Smith 5-0; Jay Bellamy 4-2; Charles Grant 4-1; Mike McKenzie 4-0; Josh Bullocks 3-1; Danny Clark 3-0; Scott Fujita 3-1.
EAGLES — Trent Cole 8-1; Roderick Hood 6-0; Sean Considine 5-4; Omar Gaither 5-1; Dhani Jones 5-3; Darwin Walker 5-0.

SAINTS 27 | EAGLES 24

With the outcome no longer in doubt against Philadelphia, Coach Sean Payton leads the cheers as the Saints advanced to the NFC championship game for the first time in franchise history.

STAFF PHOTO BY MATT ROSE

Winter wonderland? Well, the setting at Soldier Field was picturesque, but the Saints, playing in their first NFC championship game, weren't able to muzzle the Bears and came up short of advancing to Super Bowl XLI in Miami.

NFC CHAMPIONSHIP GAME

CHICAGO **Bears**

39

14

TOO MUCH TO BEAR

NEW ORLEANS' MAGICAL SEASON COMES TO AN END IN CHILLY CHICAGO, BUT THE SAINTS' FIRE FROM WITHIN STILL BURNS BRIGHT

BY MIKE TRIPLETT Staff writer

The entire season was a dream, the most spectacular in the 40-year history of the New Orleans Saints.

But like most dreams, it ended all too abruptly.

The Saints were jarred awake by a ferocious Chicago Bears' defense on a winter afternoon at Soldier Field, and they never fully emerged from their dazed state in a 39-14 loss in the NFC championship game.

The Bears earned their first trip to the Super Bowl in 21 years, but they didn't know anything about droughts.

As magical as it was, the Saints' 40th season ended the same way as all the others.

Even afterward, they were mired in that hazy fog. Not angry, not tearful. Just stunned, as they tried to come to grips with the suddenness of it all.

"It's tough when you play in the postseason, the finality of a loss stings. Especially with the season we had," Saints Coach Sean Payton said. "All of our players, it's probably the best team I've been around in terms of togetherness and guys caring about team first. I think it makes it hurt that much more.

"So we'll get back to New Orleans and begin the off-season and begin all the things you have to do to get ourselves back in the position we were in tonight."

Said running back Deuce McAllister: "Right now it stings. It hurts. I guess after a couple weeks you'll go back and look at it and you'll see just the enthusiasm and the support that our fans showed.

"We're a young team, we're going to continue to grow, we're going to get better as a team. And hopefully we'll be back at this point again."

The weather was not a huge factor. A light snow draped the field for most of the game, but it was the Saints who buried themselves in an avalanche of mistakes.

They lost the turnover battle 4-0 — two fumbles in the first quarter by receiver Marques Colston and kickoff returner Michael Lewis to help the Bears run up a 16-0 lead, then a fumble and an interception by quarterback Drew Brees in the fourth quarter as Chicago broke the game open.

With New Orleans opting to pass more than run against Chicago, quarterback Drew Brees feels the heat from nose tackle Tank Johnson on a cold and blustery day. Brees completed 27 of 49 passes for 354 yards with two touchdowns and one interception.

STAFF PHOTO BY SCOTT THRELKELD

138

BEARS 39 | SAINTS 14

Brees threw a few more errant passes than usual early in the game, and he was flagged for intentional grounding from his end zone in the third quarter, giving the Bears a safety.

But everyone was off.

The running game was grounded by the Bears' frequent use of eight men close to the line of scrimmage. Receivers dropped passes. Uncharacteristic penalties set the Saints back.

"I don't think we can blame it on the weather," Brees said, though he did insist that one of the lessons he learned was the importance of earning home-field advantage in the playoffs. "This (Bears) defense led the league in getting turnovers during the regular season. We made an emphasis the entire week of tucking the ball away — 'Don't let them yank it away' — and sure enough it happened to us four times today."

Said offensive tackle Jon Stinchcomb: "If you play in a championship game, you can't play the way we did. (The Bears) are a great team. But we did not play well. I did not play well.

"We knew what we had to do today, and we didn't do it."

The Saints' offense finally got off the ground with a hurry-up touchdown drive in the final minutes before halftime, ending in Brees' 13-yard touchdown pass to Colston.

The momentum carried over into the third quarter, when Reggie Bush scored on a sensational 88-yard touchdown pass — the longest play in NFC championship game history.

But that was it — a brief spark on the darkest day of the Saints' season.

The Saints had a chance to take a one-point lead when Billy Cundiff attempted a 47-yard field goal. But Cundiff, who had a stronger leg than teammate John Carney, missed it short.

The safety came on the Saints' next offensive possession, giving the Bears an 18-14 edge.

Then much-maligned Bears quarterback Rex Grossman delivered the biggest throw of his career — a 33-yard touchdown pass to Bernard Berrian early in the fourth quarter, giving Chicago a 25-14 lead.

And two plays later, Brees was sacked by Adewale Ogunleye, who stripped the ball away, helping to set up a Cedric Benson touchdown run.

"When we came into the locker room at halftime it was, 'Hey, we're about to explode here. We're about to blow this thing wide open,' " Brees said. "We really felt that way. So we kind of made our surge, and then they kind of obviously made theirs in the fourth quarter — and that's what won it for them."

140

New Orleans comes out fighting against Chicago in the third quarter, scoring quickly on an 88-yard pass from Drew Brees to Reggie Bush, who didn't resist strutting his stuff following the score.

TEAM	1ST	2ND	3RD	4TH	FINAL
SAINTS	0	7	7	0	14
BEARS	3	13	2	21	39

ATTENDANCE — 61,817 AT SOLDIER FIELD

SCORING SUMMARY

BEARS   Robbie Gould 19-yard field goal. Eleven plays, 35 yards in 4:44.

BEARS   Gould 43-yard field goal. Four plays, 5 yards in 1:53.

BEARS   Gould 24-yard field goal. Eight plays, 43 yards in 3:25.

BEARS   Thomas Jones 2-yard run (Gould kick). Eight plays, 69 yards in 3:55.

SAINTS   Marques Colston 13-yard pass from Drew Brees (John Carney kick). Eight plays, 73 yards in 1:10.

SAINTS   Reggie Bush 88-yard pass from Brees (Carney kick). Two plays, 93 yards in 0:53.

BEARS   Safety. Brees called for intentional grounding in the end zone.

BEARS   Bernard Berrian 33-yard pass from Rex Grossman (Gould kick). Five plays, 85 yards in 2:24.

BEARS   Cedric Benson 12-yard run (Gould kick). Four plays, 26 yards in 2:04.

BEARS   Jones 15-yard run (Gould kick). Five plays, 30 yards in 3:02.

TEAM STATISTICS	SAINTS	BEARS
FIRST DOWNS	15	18
RUSHES-YARDS (NET)	12-56	46-196
PASSING YARDS (NET)	319	144
PASSES (ATT-COMP-INT)	27-49-1	11-26-0
TOTAL OFFENSIVE PLAYS-YARDS	64-375	72-340
FUMBLES-LOST	4-3	1-0
PUNTS (NUMBER-AVG)	5-38.8	7-47.4
PUNT RETURNS-YARDS	4-15	2-24
KICKOFF RETURNS-YARDS	7-132	3-39
PENALTY YARDS	7-47	1-5
POSSESSION TIME	24:45	35:15
SACKED (YARDS LOST)	3-35	0-0
FIELD GOALS (ATT-MADE)	0-1	3-3

INDIVIDUAL OFFENSIVE STATISTICS

RUSHING   **SAINTS — Reggie Bush 4-19; Deuce McAllister 6-18; Mike Karney 1-11; Drew Brees 1-8.**
BEARS — Thomas Jones 19-123; Cedric Benson 24-60; Rashied Davis 1-16; Rex Grossman 2-minus-3.

PASSING   **SAINTS — Drew Brees 27/49-2-1, 354.**
BEARS — Rex Grossman 11/26-1-0, 144.

RECEIVING   **SAINTS — Reggie Bush 7-132; Marques Colston 5-63; Devery Henderson 2-57; Billy Miller 4-31; Terrance Copper 3-29; Deuce McAllister 3-27; Mark Karney 1-9; Mark Campbell 2-6.**
BEARS — Bernard Berrian 5-85; Desmond Clark 1-30; Muhsin Muhammad 1-20; Jason McKie 3-6; John Gilmore 1-3.

INDIVIDUAL DEFENSIVE STATISTICS

INTERCEPTIONS   **SAINTS — none. BEARS — Nathan Vasher 1.**

SACKS   **SAINTS — none. BEARS — Mark Anderson 1; Israel Idonijie 1; Adewale Ogunleye 1.**

TACKLES   **SAINTS — Scott Fujita 9-1; Jay Bellamy 7-2; Scott Shanle 6-0;**
(unassisted-   **Will Smith 6-0; Brian Young 6-1; Mark Simoneau 5-1.**
assisted)   **BEARS — Chris Harris 8-1; Lance Briggs 5-0; Nathan Vasher 5-0; Charles Tillman 4-0; Brian Urlacher 4-0.**

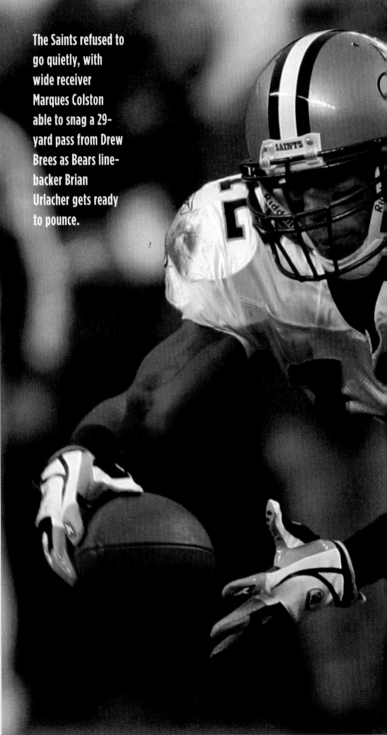

The Saints refused to go quietly, with wide receiver Marques Colston able to snag a 29-yard pass from Drew Brees as Bears linebacker Brian Urlacher gets ready to pounce.

STAFF PHOTO BY MICHAEL DEMOCKER

BEARS 39 | SAINTS 14

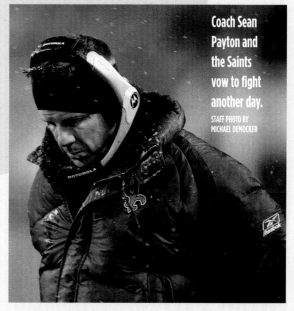

Coach Sean Payton and the Saints vow to fight another day.
STAFF PHOTO BY MICHAEL DEMOCKER

Brees stayed positive after his performance — 27-of-49 passing for 354 yards, two touchdowns, one interception, one fumble.

Like most of his teammates, he regretted that the Saints were never really able to execute their game plan — both because the Bears' defense took it away and the scoreboard eventually dictated it.

But he spoke optimistically about the future and of how this emptiness will motivate the Saints that much more over the next 12 months.

"Any time you're one game away from going to the Super Bowl, you look back on the season and obviously it's been a long one. You hope to be able to make that jump and get in the Super Bowl," Brees said. "But I can say that from where we started a year ago to now. I don't think anybody in this room, probably in America, thought that we'd be here. So I think we have a lot to be proud of.

"Although we're very disappointed that we weren't able to finish it the way that we wanted to, I think we have a lot to build on. We have a lot of young players. We have a lot of players that are just going to continue to get better. I feel like we have a great team. I'm excited as heck about the future."

Down but not out

FOR SAINTS' FANS, THE GOOD FIGHT CERTAINLY IS WORTH ALL THE PAIN

Chris Rose

There was no joy in Floodville. The Mighty Saints struck out.

No matter how much you believed, how much faith you had, how much you thought the weather wouldn't matter (and it did, big time), you had to know in the back of your mind that it wasn't to be.

It simply couldn't be. Stories that perfect never happened in real life. And if anyone knows about reality — and the lack thereof — it was us.

It was the stuff of fiction, a story of the worst team in the NFL from a stricken city somehow rising to the occasion — Against all odds! Miracle at the Midway! — to bring unity, magic and light into the darkness of the postdiluvian landscape and its people.

Real life never unfolded with the élan of a perfect Hollywood ending; scriptwriters do that, and then it always said at the end: Based on a true story.

That was us. We were based on a true story.

And a pretty damn good story. An exhilarating ride. A shot in the arm. A reason to believe.

Before New Orleans' game against the Chicago Bears, a friend called me from Kansas City, Mo., to tell me not to worry: "Yours is a team of Destiny, my friend."

But a date with Destiny always was a dangerous tryst; she was a fickle ally, a bewitching lover.

And she now lived in Chicago.

But New Orleans should be proud. Her fans represented her well. There were thousands of Saints fans who made the trip to Chicago, and they were loud and proud and ready for bear. Unfortunately, the team was not.

The lesson learned during the NFC championship game was anything a mother could have told you: When it was cold outside, wear long sleeves. And if you were going to taunt the opponent — which you shouldn't, but if you were going to — you sure as hell shouldn't do it (Reggie Bush) when the team still was trailing.

But so it went.

Bless You Boys for the effort. Good on ya!

Hundreds of thousands of friends, family and strangers in south Louisiana and Mississippi and spread across the country — together but apart — got to take a carnival ride that was well worth the price.

Two more weeks of fantasy and a spot in Super Bowl XLI in Miami would have been great — better than great; there was not even a word for it — but there always was the promise of next season, and New Orleans would celebrate in the streets soon enough, for Mardi Gras and all the other stuff we do and things we embraced.

We know how to carry on.

It cost each of us a little disappointment and maybe some tears. The game was over, but the pride carried over. It was baby steps for New Orleans; that was the way it has been since, well . . . since you know when.

My personal motto since Aug. 29, 2005, was: Keep your chin up; it gives the enemy a bigger target. Come on — hit me.

Just hit me again.

As I composed this I was sitting in an empty press box watching big flakes fall over a deserted stadium and its big green field — no field of dreams on this day for the Saints. I tried to conjure the spirits of the wizened scribes of the past to find the words to capture the season we just witnessed and to lay out the healing in print.

That was how it used to go at daily newspapers after big games like the New Orleans-Chicago contest, games that meant something. I wanted to channel Grantland Rice, Ring Lardner, Damon Runyon or some other cat like that and lay out some kind of poetry that said it all just right.

But words failed me.

I didn't even come up with the "Floodville" line. My friend, Mike Gio, in New Orleans text-messaged me that line at the end of the game.

I did see some poetry that told a little bit of the story, though. It was carved into a pillar of the old Soldier Field — preserved in the stadium's recent renovation, the words of the poet Gwendolyn Brooks:

"I swear to keep the dead upon my mind
Disdain for all time to be overglad
Among spring flowers, under summer trees
By chilling autumn waters in the frosts
At supercilious winter — all my days

BEARS 39 | SAINTS 14

When it comes to setbacks, New Orleans fans are used to them — on and off the field. Following Hurricane Katrina, fans in the deep South have embraced the Saints and their own sense of purpose with a renewed vigor — not easily put out by a defeat on a football field.

STAFF PHOTO BY MICHAEL DEMOCKER

I'll have as mentors those reproving ghosts"

That certainly put things into perspective. OK, it was a little heavy for a sporting event, but remember: This monument was called Soldier Field. The flags fly at half-mast.

For the reproving ghosts of our recent past — How many were there, 2,000? More? Do those who died of a broken heart count? — we picked up from here and moved on.

What did you do now that it was over? Simple: You get out of bed, and you go to work because there was a lot of work to do. It was our obligation and our desire.

No quit, no surrender. Not on the football field, and not in our battered and beautiful city.

We haven't, and we won't — because we can't.

145

HOT FUN IN THE SUMMERTIME? NOPE, BUT IT PAVES THE WAY FOR THE SAINTS

BY MIKE TRIPLETT Staff writer

Around Saints camp, "Millsaps" was a four-letter word.

Millsaps College was home to the Saints' grueling, month-long training camp in Jackson, Miss., last summer. A relentless series of two-a-day practices in the searing heat, with the sun and the new head coach refusing to let up.

Mention it now, and players still cringe.

"I don't even want to hear that word," said cornerback Jason Craft, who called it the toughest camp experience of his eight-year career, which included a stint with Tom Coughlin in Jacksonville.

"Actually, I think I'm still feeling a little bit from it," Craft said, though he did admit that Millsaps was "the beginning of what's going on right now."

Others were not even willing to offer that much praise.

"I will never, ever give Millsaps credit," offensive lineman Jamar Nesbit insisted. "Just in case they try to bring us back."

The Saints almost certainly will return to the small campus in downtown Jackson for training camp in 2007 — another thought that makes the players cringe — because Millsaps was indeed the birthplace of their remarkable 2006 season, an NFC South Division title and a first-round playoff bye.

That's where Coach Sean Payton took a revamped roster and an all-new staff of assistants, and together they rebuilt a team that went 3-13 in 2005.

Payton understood that such a rigorous training camp might be unpopular with players, but he never considered the decision a gamble, and he never really considered any other alternatives.

"Well, where else were you going?" said Payton, who was selected the NFL's Coach of the Year on January 6, 2007. "In other words, you were 3-13 last year. And, obviously, a lot went into the season before, besides just the record. But I think that it was a way just to begin to lay a foundation.

"So, it's not like we were taking a team that had just had a bunch of success to Millsaps to try to change things up or liven things up. We just felt like we needed

STAFF PHOTO BY SCOTT THRELKELD

SAINTS CAMP

JULY -AUG. 2006 | JACKSON, MISS. | MILLSAPS COLLEGE

With new faces dotting the scene at Millsaps College in Jackson, Miss., Coach Sean Payton, foreground, and the players gather to begin a new chapter in Saints' history. After a grueling month of conditioning and installing a new system, New Orleans had put in the work and was ready to prove doubters wrong.

With temperatures soaring during training camp at Millsaps College, defensive tackle Hollis Thomas suffers through another practice in Jackson, Miss. By season's end, Saints players said training camp only made them stronger.

STAFF PHOTO BY SUSAN POAG

to — and I think our players felt the same way — we needed to go somewhere without distraction and work on a lot of the little things.

"And it's not always easy, and it's not always something that is comfortable. But we were going to have a tough camp, and we were going to be demanding. And those were things that we were going to later draw

from, and we're able to now."

Veteran defensive tackle Hollis Thomas, as usual, had the wittiest wisecrack of training camp, on a day when Payton surprised the team with a day off at a local water park.

"I came over here just like every other day, hoping to get struck by some lightning on the way to the complex," Thomas said then. "It didn't happen, as usual."

But now, Thomas said he can sing the praises of a training camp that covered both of his feet in blisters and dropped his weight as low as 319 pounds — nearly 20 pounds lower than his playing weight.

"What it does is it weeds out the people that don't really want to be here," Thomas said. "He's not trying to break you or anything. He's just trying to put you in the best possible position you can be in. Once you realize that, it makes things easier."

Payton's training camp approach was not surprising.

The veteran players had seen it before — a first-year coach trying to establish himself as the boss, trying to establish discipline along with mental and physical toughness.

Craft said it was similar when Jack Del Rio took over in Jacksonville. Receiver Joe Horn said it was reminiscent of former Saints Coach Jim Haslett's early camps in Thibodaux.

The Saints trained in Thibodaux from 2000-2002 before staying home at the team's practice facility from 2003-2005.

"Thibodaux wasn't easy. It was hot. Very hot," said Horn, who also experienced some of Coach Marty Schottenheimer's notorious training camps in Kansas City. "I don't think a lot of guys here had ever been in a training camp of that nature. But it was a good thing. It made guys mentally tough.

"Coach Payton was new, and I think he wanted to put his foot on the ground and establish that this was a new beginning. In this profession, you don't do that by making things easy. It has to be hard."

Nesbit said players understood Payton's intentions, but there was a natural amount of skepticism to see how things would work out.

"Just one of those things where, as a player, you think that you can get the work done without bashing your head into a brick wall 90 times a practice, two times a day," Nesbit said. "As a player, you have in your mind that maybe 45 times a day is enough, maybe 30. Maybe once a day instead of twice a day.

"But, you know, when you have a season like we're having, it makes having gone through that worth it."

Sure, there was the usual amount of griping from players, but never to the point where anyone became a distraction.

In fact, the experience bonded the players. Players who have joined the team since Millsaps still get teased for having it easy.

"Those lucky guys that came in afterward," Nesbit said. "We mess with (backup lineman Rob) Petitti about it a little bit. Now, he went through camp with (Bill) Parcells, so we don't know exactly what he did.

"But he didn't go through Millsaps."

Cornerback Fred Thomas remembers his worst Millsaps moment, when he missed a day of practice because of severe cramping.

"My mind was saying no, and my body was telling me no also," Thomas said. "You usually have one or the other saying, 'Yeah, you can do it.' "

But the end result of training camp was a well-conditioned team, and the results were evident early in the season.

The Saints won their first three games against Cleveland, Green Bay and Atlanta. Defensive tackle Brian Young said in September that he felt like he and his teammates were in better condition than ever.

As the year wore on, players said they felt mentally tougher, too, which helped in come-from-behind wins over Tampa Bay and Philadelphia, among others.

"I think the biggest thing was becoming tougher," Payton said of his training camp goal. "I think you become a little bit more mentally tough, and you like to think that when you put that much time and energy into something, it's a little harder to ever let go when things aren't going well.

"We've played pretty well from behind this year. Some of that you hope is a result of training camp. Some of it has to do with your personnel, your players, your quarterback. You just try to create a toughness about your team, and that's a credit to them."

Clearly, Payton has established that toughness in the Saints. He filled his roster with the right players. He established the right attitude and philosophy.

And he whipped his team into shape at Millsaps — whether they liked it or not.

"He always let us know every day that as we go on, we'll start to see a little bit of light at the end of the tunnel," Fred Thomas said. "And as we went on, we started getting better, and guys started competing a little bit more and jelling together.

"If you look at it now and see how things turned out, you've got to tip your hat to the guy. He knew what he was talking about, and he put us in this position."

2006 FLASHBACK

FINAL NFL REGULAR SEASON STANDINGS

NFC SOUTH

TEAM	W-L	PCT.	PF	PA	HOME	ROAD	AFC	NFC	DIV.
YZ-SAINTS	10-6	62.5	413	322	4-4	6-2	1-3	9-3	4-2
PANTHERS	8-8	50.0	270	305	4-4	4-4	2-2	6-6	5-1
FALCONS	7-9	43.8	292	328	3-5	4-4	2-2	5-7	3-3
BUCCANEERS	4-12	25.0	211	353	3-5	1-7	2-2	2-10	0-6

NFC NORTH

TEAM	W-L	PCT.	PF	PA	HOME	ROAD	AFC	NFC	DIV.
*YZ BEARS	13-3	81.2	427	255	6-2	7-1	2-2	11-1	5-1
PACKERS	8-8	50.0	301	366	3-5	5-3	1-3	7-5	5-1
VIKINGS	6-10	37.5	282	327	3-5	3-5	0-4	6-6	2-4
LIONS	3-13	18.8	305	398	2-6	1-7	1-3	2-10	0-6/

NFC EAST

TEAM	W-L	PCT.	PF	PA	HOME	ROAD	AFC	NFC	DIV.
Y-EAGLES	10-6	62.5	398	328	5-3	5-3	1-3	9-3	5-1
X-COWBOYS	9-7	56.2	425	350	4-4	5-3	3-1	6-6	2-4
X-GIANTS	8-8	50.0	355	362	3-5	5-3	1-3	7-5	4-2
REDSKINS	5-11	31.2	307	376	3-5	2-6	2-2	3-9	1-5

NFC WEST

TEAM	W-L	PCT.	PF	PA	HOME	ROAD	AFC	NFC	DIV.
Y-SEAHAWKS	9-7	56.2	335	341	5-3	4-4	2-2	7-5	3-3
RAMS	8-8	.500	367	381	4-4	4-4	2-2	6-6	2-4
49ERS	7-9	43.8	298	412	4-4	3-5	2-2	5-7	3-3
CARDINALS	5-11	31.2	314	389	3-5	2-6	0-4	5-7	4-2

X-CLINCHED PLAYOFF BERTH; Y-CLINCHED DIVISION TITLE; Z-CLINCHED FIRST-ROUND BYE; *-CLINCHED HOME-FIELD ADVANTAGE

AFC SOUTH

TEAM	W-L	PCT.	PF	PA	HOME	ROAD	AFC	NFC	DIV.
Y-COLTS	12-4	75.0	427	360	8-0	4-4	9-3	3-1	3-3
TITANS	8-8	50.0	324	400	4-4	4-4	5-7	3-1	4-2
JAGUARS	8-8	50.0	371	274	6-2	2-6	5-7	3-1	2-4
TEXANS	6-10	37.5	267	366	4-4	2-6	6-6	0-4	3-3

AFC NORTH

TEAM	W-L	PCT.	PF	PA	HOME	ROAD	AFC	NFC	DIV.
YZ-RAVENS	13-3	81.2	353	201	7-1	6-2	10-2	3-1	5-1
BENGALS	8-8	50.0	373	331	4-4	4-4	6-6	2-2	4-2
STEELERS	8-8	50.0	353	315	5-3	3-5	5-7	3-1	3-3
BROWNS	4-12	25.0	238	356	2-6	2-6	3-9	1-3	0-6

AFC EAST

TEAM	W-L	PCT.	PF	PA	HOME	ROAD	AFC	NFC	DIV.
Y-PATRIOTS	12-4	75.0	385	237	5-3	7-1	8-4	4-0	4-2
X-JETS	10-6	62.5	316	295	4-4	6-2	7-5	3-1	4-2
BILLS	7-9	43.8	300	311	4-4	3-5	5-7	2-2	3-3
DOLPHINS	6-10	37.5	260	283	4-4	2-6	3-9	3-1	1-5

AFC WEST

TEAM	W-L	PCT.	PF	PA	HOME	ROAD	AFC	NFC	DIV.
*YZ-CHARGERS	14-2	87.5	492	303	8-0	6-2	10-2	4-0	5-1
X-CHIEFS	9-7	56.2	331	315	6-2	3-5	5-7	4-0	4-2
BRONCOS	9-7	56.2	319	305	4-4	5-3	8-4	1-3	3-3
RAIDERS	2-14	12.5	168	332	2-6	0-8	1-11	1-3	0-6

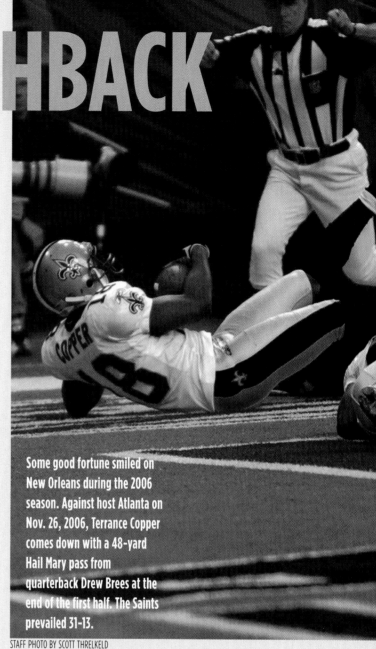

Some good fortune smiled on New Orleans during the 2006 season. Against host Atlanta on Nov. 26, 2006, Terrance Copper comes down with a 48-yard Hail Mary pass from quarterback Drew Brees at the end of the first half. The Saints prevailed 31-13.

STAFF PHOTO BY SCOTT THRELKELD

SAINTS FINAL REGULAR SEASON STATISTICS

CATEGORY	SAINTS	OPPONENTS
TOTAL FIRST DOWNS	330	262
FIRST DOWNS (RUSHING-PASSING-BY PENALTY)	99-207- 24	96-148-18
THIRD-DOWN CONVERSIONS	105/234	69/199
FOURTH-DOWN CONVERSIONS	12/20	6/13
TOTAL OFFENSIVE YARDS	6,264	4,917
OFFENSE (PLAYS-AVERAGE YARDS)	1,075-5.8	930-5.3
TOTAL RUSHING YARDS	1,761	2,063
RUSHING (PLAYS-AVERAGE YARDS)	472-3.7	418-4.9
TOTAL PASSING YARDS	4,503	2,854
PASSING (COMP-ATT-INT-AVG)	372-580-13-7.98	267-474-11-6.59
SACKS	38	23
FIELD GOALS	23/26	14/18
TOUCHDOWNS	49	40
TDS (RUSH-PASS-RETURNS-DEF)	19-27-1-0	10-26-0-4
TIME OF POSSESSION	31:53	28:07

INDIVIDUAL DEFENSIVE STATISTICS

Player	Total	Tackles	Assists	Sacks	Fum rec
Scott Shanle	97	73.0	24	4	0
Scott Fujita	96	64.0	32	3.5	0
Josh Bullocks	71	56.0	15	0	0
Charles Grant	64	49.0	15	6	2
Mark Simoneau	61	33.0	28	1	0
Omar Stoutmire	56	44.0	12	0	0
Fred Thomas	55	48.0	7	0	0
Will Smith	49	31.0	18	10.5	1
Jason Craft	47	43.0	4	0	0
Brian Young	46	36.0	10	5.5	1
Hollis Thomas	43	35.0	8	3.5	1
Mike McKenzie	33	28.0	5	0	0
Danny Clark	29	23.0	6	0	0
Roman Harper	26	24.0	2	1	0
Terrence Melton	24	17.0	7	0	1
Rodney Leisle	16	8.0	8	0	1
Jay Bellamy	16	12.0	4	0	0
Steve Gleason	16	15.0	1	0	0
DeJuan Groce	16	15.0	1	0	0
Bryan Scott	15	12.0	3	0	0
Willie Whitehead	13	9.0	4	1	0
Josh Cooper	10	8.0	2	1	0
Antwan Lake	9	8.0	1	1	0
Alfred Fincher	9	6.0	3	0	0
Curtis Deloatch	9	8.0	1	0	0
Aaron Stecker	9	7.0	2	0	0
Jamal Jones	8	6.0	2	0	1
Michael Lewis	6	5.0	1	0	1
Terrance Copper	5	4.0	1	0	1
Eric Moore	5	4.0	1	0	0
Trevor Johnson	4	3.0	1	0	0
Fred McAfee	4	4.0	0	0	0
Rob Ninkovich	4	2.0	2	0	0
Kevin Houser	3	3.0	0	0	0
Corey McIntyre	3	3.0	0	0	0
Jonathan Stinchcomb	3	3.0	0	0	1
Keith Joseph	2	2.0	0	0	0
Deuce McAllister	2	2.0	0	0	2
Steven Weatherford	2	2.0	0	0	0
Jammal Brown	2	2.0	0	0	1
Reggie Bush	2	2.0	0	0	1
Mark Campbell	1	1.0	0	0	0
Marques Colston	1	1.0	0	0	0
Devery Henderson	1	1.0	0	0	0
Joe Horn	1	1.0	0	0	0
John Owens	1	1.0	0	0	0
Zach Strief	1	1.0	0	0	0
Saints	**1,022**	**791.0**	**231**	**38**	**20**
Opponents	**1,146**	**927.0**	**219**	**23.0**	**19**

INTERCEPTIONS

Player	No.	Yds	Avg	Long	TD
Josh Bullocks	2	14	7	14	0
Scott Fujita	2	19	9	19	0
Mike McKenzie	2	54	27	54	0
Omar Stoutmire	2	10	5	10	0
Jason Craft	1	0	0	0	0
Mark Simoneau	1	0	0	0	0
Fred Thomas	1	9	9	9	0
Saints	**11**	**106**	**9**	**54**	**0**
Opponents	13	180	13	52	4

INDIVIDUAL OFFENSIVE STATISTICS (AS OF DECEMBER 31, 2006)

RUSHING

Player	No.	Yds	Avg	Long	TD
Deuce McAllister	244	1,057	4.3	57	10
Reggie Bush	155	565	3.6	18	6
Mike Karney	11	33	3.0	8	1
Drew Brees	42	32	0.8	16	0
Jamaal Branch	10	29	2.9	9	0
Devery Henderson	2	14	7.0	11	1
Fred McAfee	3	12	4.0	6	1
Aaron Stecker	4	11	2.8	4	0
Terrance Copper	1	8	8.0	8	0

PASSING

Player	Att	Comp	Yds	Pct	TD	INT	Long	Sack/lost
Drew Brees	554	356	4,418	64.3	26	11	86	18/105
Jamie Martin	24	16	208	66.7	1	1	65	5/18
Reggie Bush	1	0	0	0.0	0	1	0	0/0
Joe Horn	1	0	0	0.0	0	0	0	0/0

RECEIVING

Player	No.	Yds	Avg	Long	TD
Marques Colston	70	1,038	14.8	86	8
Devery Henderson	32	745	23.3	76	5
Reggie Bush	88	742	8.4	74	2
Joe Horn	37	679	18.4	72	4
Terrance Copper	23	385	16.7	48	3
Deuce McAllister	30	198	6.6	24	0
Aaron Stecker	19	190	10.0	48	0
Mark Campbell	18	164	9.1	33	0
Billy Miller	14	129	9.2	22	0
Jamal Jones	6	108	18.0	41	1
Mike Karney	15	96	6.4	12	2
Ernie Conwell	8	57	7.1	15	1
John Owens	4	44	11.0	25	0
Nate Lawrie	1	17	17.0	17	0

FIELD GOALS

Player	1-29	20-29	30-39	40-49	50-plus
John Carney	1/1	9/9	7/8	5/6	1/1
Billy Cundiff	0/0	0/0	0/0	0/0	0/1
Saints	1/1	9/9	7/8	5/6	1/2
Opponent	1/1	7/8	5/6	1/3	0/0

PUNTING

Player	No.	Avg	Net	TB	Inside 20	Long	Blocked
Steven Weatherford	77	43.8	37.5	10	19	59	0
Saints	**77**	**43.8**	**37.5**	**10**	**19**	**59**	**1**
Opponents	95	44.0	38.0	8	30	65	0

PUNT RETURNS

Player	Ret	FC	Yds	Avg	Long	TD
Reggie Bush	28	2	216	7.7	65	1
Michael Lewis	16	10	111	6.9	26	0
Jay Bellamy	1	0	0	0	0	0
Saints	**51**	**14**	**372**	**7.3**	**65**	**1**
Opponents	40	17	279	7.0	31	0

KICKOFF RETURNS

Player	No.	Yds	Avg	Long	TD
Michael Lewis	37	914	24.7	51	0
Aaron Stecker	10	216	21.6	31	0
Jamal Jones	6	130	21.7	29	0
Terrance Copper	4	79	19.8	25	0
Fred McAfee	1	20	20.0	20	0
Mike Karney	1	10	10.0	10	0
Antwan Lake	1	8	8.0	8	0
Saints	**60**	**1,377**	**23.0**	**51**	**0**
Opponents	72	1,598	22.2	40	0

SAINTS ROSTER

No.	Player	Pos	Ht	Wt	Exp	College
20	Jay Bellamy	S	5-11	200	13	Rutgers
9	Drew Brees	QB	6-0	209	6	Purdue
70	Jammal Brown	T	6-6	313	2	Oklahoma
29	Josh Bullocks	S	6-1	207	2	Nebraska
25	Reggie Bush	RB	6-0	203	R	Southern California
80	Mark Campbell	TE	6-6	260	9	Michigan
3	John Carney	K	5-11	185	17	Notre Dame
54	Danny Clark	LB	6-2	245	7	Illinois
12	Marques Colston	WR	6-4	231	R	Hofstra
97	Josh Cooper	DE	6-3	265	R	Ole Miss
18	Terrance Copper	WR	6-0	207	3	East Carolina
21	Jason Craft	CB	5-10	187	8	Colorado State
4	Billy Cundiff	K	6-1	201	4	Drake
39	Curtis Deloatch	CB	6-2	210	3	North Carolina A&T
73	Jahri Evans	G	6-4	318	R	Bloomsburg
52	Jeff Faine	C	6-3	291	4	Notre Dame
56	Alfred Fincher	LB	6-1	238	2	Connecticut
55	Scott Fujita	LB	6-5	250	5	California
37	Steve Gleason	S	5-11	212	6	Washington State
76	Jonathan Goodwin	OL	6-3	318	5	Michigan
94	Charles Grant	DE	6-3	290	5	Georgia
28	DeJuan Groce	CB	5-10	192	4	Nebraska
19	Devery Henderson	WR	5-11	200	3	LSU
61	Montrae Holland	G	6-2	322	4	Florida State
87	Joe Horn	WR	6-1	213	11	Itawamba (Miss.) J.C.
47	Kevin Houser	LS	6-2	252	7	Ohio State
95	Trevor Johnson	DB	6-4	260	3	Nebraska
89	Jamal Jones	WR	5-11	205	R	North Carolina A&T
44	Mike Karney	FB	5-11	258	3	Arizona State
96	Antwan Lake	DT	6-4	308	4	West Virginia
77	Rodney Leisle	DT	6-3	315	3	UCLA
84	Michael Lewis	WR	5-8	173	6	-
10	Jamie Martin	QB	6-2	205	12	Weber State
26	Deuce McAllister	RB	6-1	232	6	Ole Miss
34	Mike McKenzie	CB	6-0	194	8	Memphis
51	Terrence Melton	LB	6-1	235	3	Rice
83	Billy Miller	TE	6-3	252	7	Southern California
67	Jamar Nesbit	G	6-4	328	8	South Carolina
86	John Owens	TE	6-3	255	4	Notre Dame
79	Rob Petitti	T	6-6	327	2	Pittsburgh
24	Bryan Scott	S	6-1	219	4	Penn State
58	Scott Shanle	LB	6-2	245	4	Nebraska
53	Mark Simoneau	LB	6-0	245	7	Kansas State
91	Will Smith	DE	6-3	282	/3	Ohio State
27	Aaron Stecker	RB	5-10	213	7	Western Illinois
78	Jon Stinchcomb	T	6-5	315	4	Georgia
23	Omar Stoutmire	S	5-11	205	10	Fresno State
64	Zach Strief	T	6-7	349	R	Northwestern
22	Fred Thomas	CB	5-9	185	11	Tennessee-Martin
99	Hollis Thomas	DT	6-0	306	11	Northern Illinois
7	Steve Weatherford	P	6-3	215	R	Illnois
98	Willie Whitehead	DE	6-3	300	8	Auburn
66	Brian Young	DT	6-2	298	7	Texas-El Paso

RESERVE/INJURED

No.	Player	Pos	Ht	Wt	Exp	College
50	James Allen	LB	6-2	245	5	Oregon State
17	Mitch Berger	P	6-4	228	12	Colorado
85	Ernie Conwell	TE	6-2	255	11	Washington
41	Roman Harper	S	6-1	200	R	Alabama
74	Augie Hoffmann	G	6-2	315	2	Boston College
33	Keith Joseph	RB	6-2	249	1	Texas A&M
75	Jermane Mayberry	G	6-4	325	11	Texas A&M-Kingsville
93	Rob Ninkovich	DE	6-2	252	R	Purdue
54	Tommy Polley	LB	6-3	230	6	Florida State
79	Jimmy Verdon	DE	6-3	280	2	Arizona State

2006 DRAFT PICKS (April 29-30)

ROUND	OVERALL SELECTION	PLAYER	POSITION	SCHOOL
1	2	Reggie Bush	RB	Southern California
2	43	Roman Harper	S	Alabama
4	108	Jahri Evans	T	Bloomsburg
5	135	Rob Ninkovich	DE	Purdue
6	171	Mike Hass	WR	Oregon State
6	174	Josh Lay	CB	Pittsburgh
7	210	Zach Strief	T	Northwestern
7	252	Marques Colston	WR	Hofstra

HONORS & AWARDS

STAFF PHOTO BY SCOTT THRELKELD

Many in the Saints organization were singled out for their efforts in 2006:

Sean Payton — AP Coach of the Year; Pro Football Writers Association Coach of the Year; NFL Alumni Coach of the Year; Pro Football Weekly Coach of the Year; Sporting News Coach of the Year; Coach of the Week (weeks 6, 14).

Drew Brees — AP first team All-Pro; Sporting News first team; Pro Bowl starter; NFC Offensive Player of the Week (weeks 9, 14); Co-Walter Payton Man of the Year; FedEx Air Player of the Year

Jammal Brown — AP first team All-Pro; Pro Bowl starter.

Will Smith — Pro Bowl starter.

Mike Karney — AP second team All-Pro; Pro Bowl alternate.

Jeff Faine — Pro Bowl alternate.

Deuce McAllister — NFC Player of the Week (week 5); Saints' Ed Block Courage Award.

Reggie Bush — Pro Football Writers Association All-Rookie team; Pro Football Weekly All-Rookie team; NFL Rookie of the Week (week 1); NFC Special Teams Player of the Week (week 5); NFC Offensive Player of the Week (week 13); NFC Rookie of the Month (December).

Marques Colston — Pro Football Writers Association All-Rookie team; Pro Football Weekly All-Rookie team; NFC Rookie of the Month (October); NFC Rookie of the Week (weeks 8, 9).

Jahri Evans — Pro Football Writers Association All-Rookie team; Pro Football Weekly All-Rookie team.

John Carney — NFC Special Teams Player of the Month (September).

Scott Fujita — NFC Defensive Player of the Week (week 3).

Mickey Loomis — Pro Football Writers Association NFL Executive of the Year; Pro Football Weekly Executive of the Year.

THE ROAD TO SUPER BOWL XLI

Before the 2006 season began, Jammal Brown (70) — the Saints' first-round draft pick in 2005 out of Oklahoma — was moved from right tackle to left tackle. The moved paid off big for New Orleans and Brown. The Saints made a historic run in the postseason, and Brown was chosen to start in the Pro Bowl.

Wild-card round Jan. 6-7, 2007	Divisional playoffs Jan. 13-14, 2007	Conference Championship Jan. 21, 2007	Super Bowl XLI Feb. 4, 2007

NFC
- (4) Seattle 21
- (5) Dallas 20
- (1) Chicago 13-3
- (4) Seattle 10-7
- (1) Chicago 39
- (3) Philadelphia 23
- (6) N.Y. Giants 20
- (2) New Orleans 27
- (3) Philadelphia 24
- (2) New Orleans 14
- (1) Chicago

AFC
- (4) New England 37
- (5) N.Y. Jets 16
- (1) San Diego 14-2
- (4) New England 13-4
- (4) New England 34
- (3) Indianapolis 23
- (6) Kansas City 8
- (2) Baltimore 6
- (3) Indianapolis 15
- (3) Indianapolis 38
- (3) Indianapolis

NFL champs

Note: At the time of publication, Super Bowl XLI had not been played.

153

FOUR HORSEMEN
OF THE NEW ORLEANS SAINTS

After a demoralizing and nomadic 3-13 post-Katrina season in 2005, three Saints rode into the city and joined veteran Deuce McAllister to bring hope to a battered city and became the No. 1 offense in the NFL in 2006.

RETURNS **247** yds

RUSHING **636** yds

RECEIVING **896** yds

⚜ Denotes touchdowns

All stats reflect regular and postseason

DREW BREES

All-Pro quarterback who led the NFL in passing yards during the regular season was team's field general.

TOUCHDOWN PASSES	**29**
POINTS SCORED	**176**
LONGEST PASS	**88 YARDS**
AVERAGE YARDS PER GAME	**279**
COMPLETIONS	**63.5%**
TOTAL YARDS	**5,015**

DEUCE McALLISTER

Saints' rushing leader was an enforcer with the ball, and he was elusive in the open field.

TOUCHDOWNS	**13**
POINTS SCORED	**78**
LONGEST RUSH	**57 YARDS**
CARRIES	**271**
TOTAL YARDS	**1,464**

REGGIE BUSH

Fleet rookie was effective in the rushing and passing games and gave defenses fits by creating matchup problems.

TOUCHDOWNS	**11**
POINTS SCORED	**66**
LONGEST RETURN	**65 YARDS**
CARRIES	**171**
RECEPTIONS	**98**
TOTAL YARDS	**1,779**

MARQUES COLSTON

Rookie wide receiver was Brees' main target with his sure hands, precise route running and big frame.

TOUCHDOWNS	**9**
POINTS SCORED	**54**
LONGEST RECEPTION	**86 YARDS**
RECEPTIONS	**80**
TOTAL YARDS	**1,156**

STAFF GRAPHIC BY DAN SWENSON

THROUGH THE YEARS

Important dates in Saints' history

1966
Nov. 1   Commissioner Pete Rozelle announces at the Ponchartrain Hotel that the NFL's 16th franchise has been awarded to New Orleans.

Dec. 25   John Mecon Jr. becomes the majority stockholder/president of the franchise..

Dec. 27   Tom Fears is named the team's first head coach.

1967
Jan. 9   The team is named the Saints.

Sept. 17   New Orleans opens the regular season against the Rams. The Saints lost 27-13

1969
Nov. 2   New Orleans snaps a six-game losing streak with a 51-42 victory against the St. Louis Cardinals. The game set an NFL record for most total touchdown passes: the Saints' Billy Kilmer and the Cardinals' Charlie Johnson each had six.

1970
Nov. 3   J.D. Roberts becomes the team's second head coach.

Nov. 8   Kicker Tom Dempsey kicks a NFL-record 63-yard field goal on the game's final play to defeat Detroit 19-17.

1971
Jan. 28   The Saints draft Ole Miss quarterback Archie Manning.

Aug. 11   Construction on the Superdome begins.

1973
Nov. 4   New Orleans has its first shutout at Tulane Stadium, defeating the Buffalo Bills 13-0. The team holds running back O.J. Simpson to his lowest rushing total ofthe season — 79 yards on 20 carries.

1974
Dec. 8   New Orleans ends its eight-season stay at Tulane Stadium with a 23-32-1 home record after a 14-0 victory over the Cardinals.

1975
Aug. 9   The Saints play their first game at the Superdome, losing to the Houston Oilers 13-7 in a preseason game.

1979
Dec. 3   Running back Chuck Muncie becomes the first Saint to surpass the 1,000-yard milestone on the way to a 1,198-yard season.

1980
Jan. 27   Five Saints are selected for the Pro Bowl, the most over for the team: Manning, Muncie, who was the game's MVP, tight end Henry Childs, safety Tommy Myers and wide receiver Wes Chandler.

1982
Sept. 17   Manning is traded to the Houston Oilers for tackle Leon Gray.

Sept. 20   NFL players go on strike, and seven games are canceled.

1983
Sept. 18   New Orleans defeats the Chicago Bears 34-31 at the Superdome for the first overtime victory in franchise history.

Dec. 18   The Saints narrowly miss the NFC playoffs when the Rams kick a 42-yard field goal with six seconds left. New Orleans finishes the season with the NFC's top-ranked overall defense and the NFL's top defense against the pass — both franchise firsts.

1984
Nov. 26   Mecom says the Saints are for sale for $75 million. Non-negotiable.

1985
March 12   Mecom agrees to sell the Saints to New Orleanian Tom Benson for about $70.2 million

1986
Jan. 28   Jim Mora is named New Orleans' 10th head coach.

Dec. 21   Saints running back Rueben Mayes finishes the season with 1,353 yards rushing (fourth in the NFL) and later is chosen the NFL's Rookie of the Year.

1987
Oct. 25   The Saints fall to San Francisco 24-22 at the Superdome. Following the game, Mora makes his "coulda, woulda, shoulda" proclamation.

Nov. 29   The Saints achieve their first winning season with a fourth quarter victory over host Pittsburgh 20-16.

1988
Jan. 3   The Minnesota Vikings end the Saints' playoff dreams with a 44-10 victory in an NFC wild-card game at the Superdome.

Feb. 7   A team-record six Saints — kicker Morten Andersen, tight end Hoby Brenner, guard Brad Edelman, linebacker Sam Mills, cornerback Dave Waymer and Mayes were chosen for the Pro Bowl. Mora is chosen NFL Coach of the Year.

1991
Dec. 22   In Phoenix, the Saints beat the Cardinals 27-3 to win their first NFC West title.

1993
May 19   State lawmakers approve a bill that in part called for renovations to the Superdome and a new practice facility for the team.

1994
May 8   After battling lung cancer, Saints president/general manager Jim Finks, who had resigned the previous summer, dies at his Metairie home. He was 66.

Oct. 23   En route to edging the Rams 37-34 at the Superdome, the Saints' Tyrone Hughes — who returned two kick offs for touchdowns — sets or ties seven team and four NFL records.

1995
Jan. 26   An early-morning fire severely damages the Saints' practice facility.

Jan. 31   Former Bills linebacker Jim Haslett is hired as linebackers coach.

June 8   Groundbreaking ceremonies are held for the Saints' new practice facility in Metairie.

1996
Jan. 30   Haslett is promoted to defensive coordinator.

Oct. 21   Following a 19-7 defeat to the Carolina Panthers a day earlier, Mora resigns as coach after 10-1/2 years.

1997
Jan. 28   Mike Ditka is tapped as the Saints' 12th head coach.

Nov. 16   In the quickest overtime game in NFL history, New Orleans beat the Seattle Seahawks 20-17 on a 38-yard field goal by Doug Brien just 17 seconds into extra time.

2000
Jan. 5   Benson fires 22 employees, including Ditka and president/general manager Bill Kuharich.

Feb. 3   Haslett is named the Saints' 13th head coach.

Dec. 18   In one year, New Orleans goes from last place to division champs by clinching the NFC West title — its second ever — after beating the Rams 38-35 in Tampa.

Dec. 30   The Saints achieve their first postseason victory against the Rams, 31-28.

2001
Sept. 30   The Saints play the first NFL game in New York after the 9/11 terror attacks, losing 21-13 to the Giants.

2003
Dec. 14   Quarterback Aaron Brooks completes a career-high five touchdowns, including a club-record four caught by wide receiver Joe Horn, in the Saints' 45-7 victory over the Giants.

2006
Jan. 2   At the conclusion of a turbulent, Katrina-marred 3-13 season, Haslett is fired.

Jan. 18   Sean Payton is named coach.

Sept. 25   The Saints play to a home crowd at the Superdome for the first time since Hurricane Katrina severely dam aged the facility 13 months earlier.

Dec. 17   New Orleans captures the NFC South title.

2007
Jan. 13   The Saints defeat the Eagles 27-24 in a playoff game and advance to the NFC championship game for the first time.

Jan. 21   New Orleans falls to the Bears 39-14 in the NFC championship game in Chicago.

— MICHAEL J. MONTALBANO

COMPLETE SCORECARD

The Saints' results over the years

1967 SAINTS: 3-11

DATE	OPPONENT	RESULT
Sept. 17	Rams	L 27-13
Sept. 24	Redskins	L 30-10
Oct. 1	Browns	L 42-7
Oct. 8	at Giants	L 27-21
Oct. 15	at Cowboys	L 14-10
Oct. 22	at 49ers	L 27-13
Oct. 29	Steelers	L 14-10
Nov. 5	Eagles	W 31-24
Nov. 12	Cowboys	L 27-10
Nov. 19	at Eagles	L 41-28
Nov. 26	Falcons	W 27-24
Dec. 3	at Cardinals	L 31-20
Dec. 10	at Colts	L 30-10
Dec. 17	at Redskins	W 30-14

COACH: **TOM FEARS**

1968 SAINTS: 4-9-1

DATE	OPPONENT	RESULT
Sept. 15	Browns	L 24-10
Sept. 22	Redskins	W 37-17
Sept. 29	Cardinals	L 21-20
Oct. 6	at Giants	L 38-21
Oct. 13	Vikings	W 20-17
Oct. 20	at Steelers	W 16-12
Oct. 27	at Cardinals	L 31-17
Nov. 3	Cowboys	L 17-3
Nov. 10	at Browns	L 35-17
Nov. 17	at Packers	L 29-7
Nov. 24	at Lions	T 20-20
Dec. 1	Bears	L 23-17
Dec. 8	at Eagles	L 29-17
Dec. 15	Steelers	W 24-14

COACH: **TOM FEARS**

1969 SAINTS: 5-9

DATE	OPPONENT	RESULT
Sept. 21	Redskins	L 26-20
Sept. 28	Cowboys	L 21-17
Oct. 5	at Rams	L 36-17
Oct. 12	Browns	L 27-17
Oct. 19	Colts	L 30-10
Oct. 26	at Eagles	L 13-10
Nov. 2	at Cardinals	W 51-42
Nov. 9	at Cowboys	L 33-17
Nov. 16	at Giants	W 25-24
Nov. 23	49ers	W 43-38
Nov. 30	Eagles	W 26-17
Dec. 7	at Falcons	L 45-17
Dec. 14	at Redskins	L 17-14
Dec. 17	Steelers	W 27-24

COACH: **TOM FEARS**

1970 SAINTS: 2-11-1

DATE	OPPONENT	RESULT
Sept. 20	Falcons	L 14-3
Sept. 27	at Vikings	L 26-0
Oct. 4	Giants	W 14-10
Oct. 11	at Cardinals	L 24-17
Oct. 18	at 49ers	T 20-20
Oct. 25	at Falcons	L 32-14
Nov. 1	Rams	L 30-17
Nov. 8	Lions	W 19-17
Nov. 15	at Dolphins	L 21-10
Nov. 22	Broncos	L 31-6
Nov. 29	at Bengals	L 26-6
Dec. 6	at Rams	L 34-16
Dec. 13	49ers	L 38-27
Dec. 20	Bears	L 24-3

COACHES: **TOM FEARS (SEVEN GAMES: 1-5-1)**, **J.D. ROBERTS (SEVEN GAMES: 1-6)**

1971 SAINTS: 4-8-2

DATE	OPPONENT	RESULT
Sept. 19	Rams	W 24-20
Sept. 26	49ers	L 38-20
Oct. 3	at Oilers	T 13-13
Oct. 10	at Bears	L 35-14
Oct. 17	Cowboys	W 24-14
Oct. 24	at Falcons	L 28-6
Oct. 31	at Redskins	L 24-14
Nov. 7	Raiders	T 21-21
Nov. 14	at 49ers	W 26-20
Nov. 21	Vikings	L 23-10
Nov. 28	at Packers	W 29-21
Dec. 5	at Rams	L 45-28
Dec. 12	Browns	L 21-17
Dec. 19	Falcons	L 24-20

COACH: **J.D. ROBERTS**

1972 SAINTS: 2-11-1

DATE	OPPONENT	RESULT
Sept. 17	at Rams	L 34-14
Sept. 25	Chiefs	L 20-17
Oct. 1	49ers	L 37-2
Oct. 8	at Giants	L 45-21
Oct. 15	Falcons	L 21-14
Oct. 22	at 49ers	T 20-20
Oct. 29	Eagles	W 21-3
Nov. 5	at Vikings	L 37-6
Nov. 12	at Falcons	L 36-20
Nov. 19	at Lions	L 27-14
Nov. 26	Rams	W 19-16
Dec. 3	at Jets	L 18-17
Dec. 10	Patriots	L 17-10
Dec. 19	Packers	L 30-20

COACH: **J.D. ROBERTS**

1973 SAINTS: 5-9

DATE	OPPONENT	RESULT
Sept. 16	Falcons	L 62-7
Sept. 24	at Cowboys	L 40-3
Sept. 30	at Colts	L 14-10
Oct. 6	Bears	W 21-16
Oct. 13	Lions	W 20-13
Oct. 20	at 49ers	L 40-0
Oct. 27	Redskins	W 19-3
Nov. 4	Bills	W 13-0
Nov. 11	at Rams	L 29-7
Nov. 18	at Chargers	L 17-14
Nov. 25	Rams	L 24-13
Dec. 2	at Packers	L 30-17
Dec. 9	49ers	W 16-10
Dec. 16	at Falcons	L 14-10

COACH: **JOHN NORTH**

1974 SAINTS: 5-9

DATE	OPPONENT	RESULT
Sept. 15	49ers	L 17-13
Sept. 22	at Rams	L 24-0
Sept. 29	Falcons	W 14-13
Oct. 6	at Bears	L 24-10
Oct. 13	at Broncos	L 33-17
Oct. 20	at Falcons	W 13-3
Oct. 27	Eagles	W 14-10
Nov. 3	at Lions	L 19-14
Nov. 10	Dolphins	W 20-7
Nov. 17	Rams	L 28-7
Nov. 25	Steelers	L 24-13
Dec. 1	at Vikings	L 29-9
Dec. 8	Cardinals	W 14-0
Dec. 15	at 49ers	L 35-21

COACH: **JOHN NORTH**

1975 SAINTS: 2-12

DATE	OPPONENT	RESULT
Sept. 21	at Redskins	L 41-3
Sept. 28	Bengals	L 21-0
Oct. 5	at Falcons	L 14-7
Oct. 12	Packers	W 20-19
Oct. 19	at 49ers	L 35-21
Oct. 26	at Rams	L 38-14
Nov. 2	Falcons	W 23-7
Nov. 9	at Raiders	L 48-10
Nov. 16	Vikings	L 20-7
Nov. 23	49ers	L 16-6
Nov. 30	at Browns	L 17-16
Dec. 7	Rams	L 14-7
Dec. 14	at Giants	L 28-14
Dec. 21	Bears	L 42-17

COACHES: **JOHN NORTH (SIX GAMES: 1-5)**, **ERNIE HEFFERLE (EIGHT GAMES: 1-7)**

1976 SAINTS: 4-10

DATE	OPPONENT	RESULT
Sept. 12	Vikings	L 40-9
Sept. 19	Cowboys	L 24-6
Sept. 26	at Chiefs	W 27-17
Oct. 3	Oilers	L 31-26
Oct. 10	Falcons	W 30-0
Oct. 17	at 49ers	L 33-3
Oct. 24	Rams	L 16-10
Oct. 31	at Falcons	L 23-20
Nov. 7	at Packers	L 32-27
Nov. 14	Lions	W 17-16
Nov. 21	at Seahawks	W 51-27
Nov. 28	at Rams	L 33-14
Dec. 5	at Patriots	L 27-6
Dec. 12	49ers	L 27-7

COACH: **HANK STRAM**

1977 SAINTS: 3-11

DATE	OPPONENT	RESULT
Sept. 18	Packers	L 24-20
Sept. 25	at Lions	L 23-19
Oct. 2	at Bears	W 42-24
Oct. 9	Cargers	L 14-0
Oct. 16	at Rams	L 14-7
Oct. 23	at Cardinals	L 49-31
Oct. 30	Rams	W 27-26
Nov. 6	at Eagles	L 28-7
Nov.13	49ers	L 10-7 OT
Nov. 20	Falcons	W 21-20
Nov. 27	at 49ers	L 20-17
Dec. 4	Jets	L 16-13
Dec. 11	Buccaneers	L 33-14
Dec. 18	at Falcons	L 35-7

COACH: **HANK STRAM**

1978 SAINTS: 7-9

DATE	OPPONENT	RESULT
Sept. 3	Vikings	W 31-24
Sept. 10	at Packers	L 28-17
Sept. 17	Eagles	L 24-17
Sept. 24	at Bengals	W 20-18
Oct. 1	Rams	L 26-20
Oct. 8	Browns	L 20-16
Oct. 15	at 49ers	W 14-7
Oct. 22	at Rams	W 10-3
Oct. 29	Giants	W 28-17
Nov. 5	at Steelers	L 20-14
Nov. 12	Falcons	L 20-17
Nov. 19	at Cowboys	L 27-7
Nov. 26	at Falcons	L 20-17
Dec. 3	49ers	W 24-13
Dec. 10	Oilers	L 17-12
Dec. 17	at Buccaneers	W 17-10

COACH: **DICK NOLAN**

1979 SAINTS: 8-8

DATE	OPPONENT	RESULT
Sept. 2	Falcons	L 40-34 OT
Sept. 9	at Packers	L 28-19
Sept. 16	Eagles	L 26-14
Sept. 23	at 49ers	W 30-21
Sept. 30	Giants	W 24-14
Oct. 7	Rams	L 35-17
Oct. 14	at Buccaneers	W 42-14
Oct. 21	Lions	W 17-7
Oct. 28	at Redskins	W 14-10
Nov. 4	at Broncos	L 10-3
Nov. 11	49ers	W 31-20
Nov. 18	at Seahawks	L 38-24
Nov. 25	at Falcons	W 37-6
Dec. 3	Raiders	L 42-35
Dec. 9	Chargers	L 35-0
Dec. 16	at Rams	W 29-14

COACH: **DICK NOLAN**

1980 SAINTS: 1-15

DATE	OPPONENT	RESULT
Sept. 7	49ers	L 26-23
Sept. 14	at Bears	L 22-3
Sept. 21	Bills	L 35-26
Sept. 28	at Dolphins	L 21-16
Oct. 5	Cardinals	L 40-7
Oct. 12	at Lions	L 24-13
Oct. 19	Falcons	L 41-14
Oct. 26	at Redskins	L 22-14
Nov. 2	at Rams	L 45-31
Nov. 9	Eagles	L 31-13
Nov. 16	at Falcons	L 24-13
Nov. 24	Rams	L 27-7
Nov. 30	Vikings	L 23-20
Dec. 7	at 49ers	L 38-35 OT
Dec. 14	at Jets	W 21-20
Dec. 21	Patriots	L 38-27

COACHES: **DICK NOLAN (12 GAMES: 0-12), DICK STANFEL (FOUR GAMES: 1-3)**

1981 SAINTS: 4-12

DATE	OPPONENT	RESULT
Sept. 6	at Falcons	L 27-0
Sept. 13	Rams	W 23-17
Sept. 20	at Giants	L 20-7
Sept. 27	at 49ers	L 21-14
Oct. 4	Steelers	L 20-6
Oct. 11	Eagles	L 31-14
Oct. 18	at Browns	L 20-17
Oct. 25	Bengals	L 17-7
Nov. 1	Falcons	L 41-10
Nov. 8	at Rams	W 21-13
Nov. 15	at Vikings	L 20-10
Nov. 22	at Oilers	L 27-7
Nov. 30	Buccaneers	W 24-27
Dec. 6	at Cardinals	L 30-3
Dec. 13	Packers	L 35-7
Dec. 20	49ers	W 21-17

COACH: **BUM PHILLIPS**

1982 SAINTS: 4-5

DATE	OPPONENT	RESULT
Sept. 12	Cardinals	L 21-7
Sept. 19	at Bears	W 10-0
Nov. 21	Chiefs	W 27-17
Nov. 28	at 49ers	W 23-20
Dec. 5	Buccaneers	L 13-10
Dec. 12	at Falcons	L 35-0
Dec. 19	at Cowboys	L 21-7
Dec. 26	Redskins	L 27-10
Jan. 2	Falcons	W 35-6

COACH: **BUM PHILLIPS**

1983 SAINTS: 8-8

DATE	OPPONENT	RESULT
Sept. 4	Cardinals	W 28-17
Sept. 11	at Rams	L 30-27
Sept. 18	Bears	W 34-31 OT
Sept. 25	at Cowboys	L 21-20
Oct. 2	Dolphins	W 17-7
Oct. 9	Falcons	W 19-17
Oct. 16	49ers	L 32-13
Oct. 23	at Buccaneers	W 24-21
Oct. 30	at Bills	L 27-21
Nov. 6	Falcons	W 27-10
Nov. 13	at 49ers	L 27-0
Nov. 20	Jets	L 31-28
Nov. 26	Vikings	W 19-17
Dec. 3	at Patriots	L 7-0
Dec. 10	at Eagles	W 20-17 OT
Dec. 17	Rams	L 26-24

COACH: **BUM PHILLIPS**

1984 SAINTS: 7-9

DATE	OPPONENT	RESULT
Sept. 2	Falcons	L 36-28
Sept. 9	Buccaneers	W 17-3
Sept. 16	at 49ers	L 30-20
Sept. 23	Cardinals	W 34-24
Sept. 30	at Oilers	W 27-10
Oct. 7	at Bears	L 20-7
Oct. 14	Rams	L 28-10
Oct. 21	at Cowboys	L 30-27 OT
Oct. 28	at Browns	W 16-14
Nov. 4	Packers	L 23-13
Nov. 11	at Falcons	W 17-13
Nov. 19	Steelers	W 27-24
Nov. 25	49ers	L 35-3
Dec. 2	at Rams	L 34-21
Dec. 9	Browns	L 24-21
Dec. 16	at Giants	W 10-3

COACH: **BUM PHILLIPS**

1985 SAINTS: 5-11

DATE	OPPONENT	RESULT
Sept. 8	Chiefs	L 47-27
Sept. 15	at Broncos	L 34-23
Sept. 22	Buccaneers	W 20-13
Sept. 29	at 49ers	W 20-17
Oct. 6	Eagles	W 23-21
Oct. 13	at Raiders	L 23-13
Oct. 20	at Falcons	L 31-24
Oct. 27	Giants	L 21-13
Nov. 3	at Rams	L 28-10
Nov. 10	Seahawks	L 27-3
Nov. 17	at Packers	L 38-14
Nov. 24	at Vikings	W 30-23
Dec. 1	Rams	W 29-3
Dec. 8	at Cardinals	L 28-16
Dec. 15	49ers	L 31-19
Dec. 22	Falcons	L 16-10

COACHES: **BUM PHILLIPS (12 GAMES: 4-8), WADE PHILLIPS (FOUR GAMES: 1-3)**

1986 SAINTS: 7-9

DATE	OPPONENT	RESULT
Sept. 7	Falcons	L 31-10
Sept. 14	Packers	W 24-10
Sept. 21	at 49ers	L 26-17
Sept. 28	at Giants	L 20-17
Oct. 5	Redskins	L 14-6
Oct. 12	at Colts	W 17-14
Oct. 19	Buccaneers	W 38-7
Oct. 26	at Jets	L 28-23
Nov. 2	49ers	W 23-10
Nov. 9	Rams	W 6-0
Nov. 16	at Cardinals	W 16-7
Nov. 23	at Rams	L 16-13
Nov. 30	Patriots	L 21-20
Dec. 7	Dolphins	L 31-27
Dec. 14	at Falcons	W 14-9
Dec. 21	at Vikings	L 33-17

COACH: **JIM MORA**

1987 SAINTS: 12-4

DATE	OPPONENT	RESULT
Sept. 13	Browns	W 28-21
Sept. 20	at Eagles	L 27-17
Oct. 4	Rams	W 37-10
Oct. 11	at Cardinals	L 24-19
Oct. 18	at Bears	W 19-17
Oct. 25	49ers	L 24-22
Nov. 1	at Falcons	W 38-0
Nov. 8	at Rams	W 31-14
Nov. 15	at 49ers	W 26-24
Nov. 22	Giants	W 23-14
Nov. 29	at Steelers	W 20-16
Dec. 6	Buccaneers	W 44-34
Dec. 13	Oilers	W 24-10
Dec. 20	at Bengals	W 41-24
Dec. 27	Packers	W 33-24

NFC WILD-CARD GAME

DATE	OPPONENT	RESULT
Jan. 3	Vikings	L 44-10

COACH: **JIM MORA**

1988 SAINTS: 10-6

DATE	OPPONENT	RESULT
Sept. 4	49ers	L 34-33
Sept. 11	at Falcons	W 29-21
Sept. 18	at Lions	W 22-14
Sept. 25	Buccaneers	W 13-9
Oct. 3	Cowboys	W 20-17
Oct. 9	at Chargers	W 23-17
Oct. 16	at Seahawks	W 20-19
Oct. 23	Raiders	W 20-6
Oct. 30	Rams	L 12-10
Nov. 6	at Redskins	L 27-24
Nov. 13	at Rams	W 14-10
Nov. 20	Broncos	W 42-0
Nov. 27	Giants	L 13-12
Dec. 4	at Vikings	L 45-3
Dec. 11	at 49ers	L 30-17
Dec. 18	Falcons	W 10-9

COACH: **JIM MORA**

1989 SAINTS: 9-7

DATE	OPPONENT	RESULT
Sept. 10	Cowboys	W 28-0
Sept. 17	at Packers	L 35-34
Sept. 25	at Buccaneers	L 20-10
Oct. 1	Redskins	L 16-14
Oct. 8	49ers	L 24-20
Oct. 15	Jets	W 29-14
Oct. 22	at Rams	W 40-21
Oct. 29	Falcons	W 20-13
Nov. 6	at 49ers	L 31-13
Nov. 12	at Patriots	W 28-24
Nov. 19	at Falcons	W 26-17
Nov. 26	Rams	L 20-17 OT
Dec. 3	at Lions	L 21-14
Dec. 10	at Bills	W 22-19
Dec. 17	Eagles	W 30-20
Dec. 24	Colts	W 41-6

COACH: **JIM MORA**

1990 SAINTS: 8-9

DATE	OPPONENT	RESULT
Sept. 10	49ers	L 13-12
Sept. 16	Vikingss	L 32-3
Sept. 23	Cardinals	W 28-17
Oct. 7	Falcons	L 28-27
Oct. 14	Browns	W 25-20
Oct. 21	Oilers	L 23-10
Oct. 28	Lions	L 27-10
Nov. 4	Bengals	W 21-7
Nov. 11	Buccaneers	W 35-7
Nov. 18	Redskins	L 31-17
Nov. 25	Falcons	W 10-7
Dec. 2	Cowboys	L 17-13
Dec. 9	Rams	W 24-20
Dec. 16	Steelers	L 9-6
Dec. 23	49ers	W 13-10
Dec. 31	Rams	W 20-17

NFC WILD-CARD GAME

DATE	OPPONENT	RESULT
Jan. 6	Bears	L 16-6

COACH: **JIM MORA**

Jim Mora had success with the Saints, but his run as head coach came to an end during the 1996 season.

1991 SAINTS: 11-6

DATE	OPPONENT	RESULT
Sept. 1	Seahawks	W 27-24
Sept. 8	at Chiefs	W 17-10
Sept. 15	Rams	W 24-7
Sept. 22	Vikings	W 26-0
Sept. 29	at Falcons	W 27-6
Oct. 13	at Eagles	W 13-6
Oct. 20	Buccaneers	W 23-7
Oct. 27	Bears	L 20-17
Nov. 3	at Rams	W 24-17
Nov. 10	49ers	W 10-3
Nov. 17	at Chargers	L 24-21
Nov. 24	Falcons	L 23-20 OT
Dec. 1	at 49ers	L 38-24
Dec. 8	at Cowboys	L 23-14
Dec. 16	Raiders	W 27-0
Dec. 22	at Cardinals	W 27-3

NFC WILD-CARD GAME

DATE	OPPONENT	RESULT
Dec. 28.	Falcons	L 27-20

COACH: **JIM MORA**

1992 SAINTS: 12-5

DATE	OPPONENT	RESULT
Sept. 6	at Eagles	L 15-13
Sept. 13	Bears	W 28-6
Sept. 20	at Falcons	W 10-7
Sept. 27	49ers	L 16-10
Oct. 4	at Lions	W 13-7
Oct. 11	Rams	W 13-10
Oct. 18	at Cardinals	W 30-21
Nov. 1	Buccaneers	W 23-21
Nov. 8	at Patriots	W 31-14
Nov. 15	at 49ers	L 21-20
Nov. 23	Redskins	W 20-3
Nov. 29	Dolphins	W 24-13
Dec. 3	Falcons	W 22-14
Dec. 13	at Rams	W 37-14
Dec. 20	Bills	L 20-16
Dec. 26	at Jets	W 20-0

NFC WILD-CARD GAME

DATE	OPPONENT	RESULT
Jan 3	Eagles	L 36-20

COACH: **JIM MORA**

1993 SAINTS: 8-8

DATE	OPPONENT	RESULT
Sept. 5	Oilers	W 33-21
Sept. 12	at Falcons	W 34-31
Sept. 19	Lions	W 14-3
Sept. 26	49ers	W 16-13
Oct. 3	at Rams	W 37-6
Oct. 17	at Steelers	L 37-14
Oct. 24	Falcons	L 26-15
Oct. 31	at Cardinals	W 20-17
Nov. 14	Packers	L 19-17
Nov. 22	at 49ers	L 42-7
Nov. 28	at Vikings	W 17-14
Dec. 5	at Browns	L 17-13
Dec. 12	Rams	L 23-20
Dec. 20	Giants	L 24-14
Dec. 26	at Eagles	L 37-26
Jan. 2	Bengals	W 20-13

COACH: **JIM MORA**

1994 SAINTS: 7-9

DATE	OPPONENT	RESULT
Sept. 4	Chiefs	L 30-17
Sept. 11	Redskins	L 38-24
Sept. 18	at Buccaneers	W 9-7
Sept. 24	at 49ers	L 24-13
Oct. 2	Giants	W 27-22
Oct. 9	at Bears	L 17-7
Oct. 16	Chargers	L 36-22
Oct. 23	Rams	W 37-34
Nov. 6	at Vikings	L 21-20
Nov. 13	Falcons	W 33-32
Nov. 20	at Raiders	L 24-19
Nov. 28	49ers	L 35-14
Dec. 4	at Rams	W 31-15
Dec. 11	at Falcons	W 29-20
Dec. 19	Cowboys	L 24-16
Dec. 24	at Broncos	W 30-28

COACH: **JIM MORA**

1995 SAINTS: 7-9

DATE	OPPONENT	RESULT
Sept. 3	49ers	L 24-22
Sept. 10	at Rams	L 17-13
Sept. 17	Falcons	L 27-24
Sept. 24	at Giants	L 45-29
Oct. 1	Eagles	L 15-10
Oct. 15	Dolphins	W 33-30
Oct. 22	at Panthers	L 20-3
Oct. 29	at 49ers	W 11-7
Nov. 5	Rams	W 19-10
Nov. 12	Colts	W 17-14
Nov. 19	at Vikings	L 43-24
Nov. 26	Panthers	W 34-26
Dec. 3	at Patriots	W 31-17
Dec. 10	at Falcons	L 19-14
Dec. 16	Packers	L 34-23
Dec. 24	at Jets	W 12-0

COACH: **JIM MORA**

1996 SAINTS: 3-13

DATE	OPPONENT	RESULT
Sept. 1	at 49ers	L 27-11
Sept. 8	Panthers	L 22-20
Sept. 15	at Bengals	L 30-15
Sept. 22	Cardinals	L 28-14
Sept. 29	at Ravens	L 17-10
Oct. 6	Jaguars	W 17-13
Oct. 13	Bears	W 27-24
Oct. 20	at Panthers	L 19-7
Nov. 3	49ers	L 24-17
Nov. 10	Oilers	L 34-14
Nov. 17	at Falcons	L 17-15
Nov. 24	at Buccaneers	L 13-7
Dec. 1	Rams	L 26-10
Dec. 8	Falcons	L 31-15
Dec. 15	at Giants	W 17-3
Dec. 28	at Rams	L 14-13

COACHES: **JIM MORA (EIGHT GAMES: 2-6),
RICK VENTURI (EIGHT GAMES: 1-7)**

1997 SAINTS: 6-10

DATE	OPPONENT	RESULT
Aug. 31	at Rams	L 38-24
Sept. 7	Chargers	L 20-6
Sept. 14	at 49ers	L 33-7
Sept. 21	Lions	W 35-17
Sept. 28	at Giants	L 14-9
Oct. 5	at Bears	W 20-17
Oct. 12	Falcons	L 23-17
Oct. 19	Panthers	L 13-0
Oct. 26	49ers	L 23-0
Nov. 9	at Raiders	W 13-10
Nov. 16	Seahawks	W 20-17
Nov. 23	at Falcons	L 20-3
Nov. 30	at Panthers	W 16-13
Dec 7	Rams	L 37-34
Dec. 14	Cardinals	W 27-10
Dec. 21	at Chiefs	L 25-13

COACH: **MIKE DITKA**

1998 SAINTS: 6-10

DATE	OPPONENT	RESULT
Sept. 6	at Rams	W 24-17
Sept.13	Panthers	W 19-14
Sept. 27	at Colts	W 19-13
Oct. 4	Patriots	L 30-27
Oct. 11	49ers	L 31-0
Oct. 18	at Falcons	L 31-23
Oct. 25	Buccaneers	W 9-3
Nov. 1	at Panthers	L 31-17
Nov. 8	at Vikings	L 31-24
Nov. 15	Rams	W 24-3
Nov. 22	at 49ers	L 31-20
Nov. 29	at Dolphins	L 30-10
Dec. 6	Cowboys	W 22-3
Dec. 13	Falcons	L 27-17
Dec. 20	at Cardinals	L 19-17
Dec. 27	Bills	L 45-33

COACH: **MIKE DITKA**

The Vikings put a halt to Chad Morton and the Saints during an NFC divisional playoff game Jan. 6, 2001, in Minneapolis.

Because of Hurricane Katrina, the Saints played the Dolphins on Oct. 30, 2006, at Tiger Stadium in Baton Rouge.

1999 SAINTS: 3-13

DATE	OPPONENT	RESULT
Sept. 12	Panthers	W 19-10
Sept. 19	at 49ers	L 28-21
Oct. 3	at Bears	L 14-10
Oct. 10	Falcons	L 20-17
Oct. 17	Titans	L 24-21
Oct. 24	at Giants	L 31-3
Oct. 31	Browns	L 21-16
Nov. 07	Buccaneers	L 31-16
Nov. 14	49ers	W 24-6
Nov. 21	at Jaguars	L 41-23
Nov. 28	at Rams	L 43-12
Dec. 5	at Falcons	L 35-12
Dec. 12	Rams	L 30-14
Dec. 19	at Ravens	L 31-8
Dec. 24	Cowboys	W 31-24
Jan. 2	at Panthers	L 45-13

COACH: **MIKE DITKA**

2000 SAINTS: 11-7

DATE	OPPONENT	RESULT
Sept. 2	Lions	L 14-10
Sept. 9	at Chargers	W 28-27
Sept. 16	at Seahawks	L 20-10
Sept. 23	Eagles	L 21-7
Oct. 8	at Bears	W 31-10
Oct. 14	Panthers	W 24-6
Oct. 21	at Falcons	W 21-19
Oct. 28	at Cardinals	W 21-10
Nov. 5	49ers	W 31-15
Nov. 12	at Panthers	W 20-10
Nov. 19	Raiders	L 31-22
Nov. 24	at Rams	W 31-24
Dec. 3	Broncos	L 38-23
Dec. 10	at 49ers	W 31-27
Dec. 17	Falcons	W 31-7
Dec. 24	Rams	L 26-21

NFC WILD-CARD GAME

DATE	OPPONENT	RESULT
Dec. 30	Rams	W 31-28

NFC DIVISIONAL PLAYOFF GAME

DATE	OPPONENT	RESULT
Jan. 6	at Vikings	L 34-16

COACH: **JIM HASLETT**

2001 SAINTS: 7-9

DATE	OPPONENT	RESULT
Sept. 9	at Bills	W 24-6
Sept. 30	at Giants	L 21-13
Oct. 7	Vikings	W 28-15
Oct. 14	at Panthers	W 27-25
Oct. 21	Falcons	L 20-13
Oct. 28	at Rams	W 31-34
Nov. 4	Jets	L 16-9
Nov. 11	at 49ers	L 28-27
Nov. 18	Colts	W 34-20
Nov. 25	at Patriots	L 34-17
Dec. 2	Panthers	W 27-23
Dec. 9	at Falcons	W 28-10
Dec. 16	Rams	L 34-21
Dec. 23	at Buccaneers	L 48-21
Dec. 30	Redskins	L 40-10
Jan. 6	49ers	L 38-0

COACH: **JIM HASLETT**

2005 SAINTS: 3-13

DATE	OPPONENT	RESULT
Sept. 11	at Panthers	W 23-20
Sept. 19	*Giants	L 27-10
Sept. 25	at Vikings	L 33-16
Oct. 2	**Bills	W 19-7
Oct. 9	at Packers	L 52-3
Oct. 16	**Falcons	L 34-31
Oct. 23	at Rams	L 28-17
Oct. 30	***Dolphins	L 21-6
Nov. 6	***Bears	L 20-17
Nov. 20	at Patriots	L 24-17
Nov. 27	at Jets	W 21-19
Dec. 4	***Buccaneers	L 10-3
Dec. 12	at Falcons	L 36-17
Dec. 18	***Panthers	L 27-10
Dec. 24	**Lions	L 13-12
Jan. 1	at Buccaneers	L 27-13

Note: New Orleans didn't play a home game at the Superdome because of Hurricane Katrina.
*In East Rutherford, N.J.
**In San Antonio
***In Baton Rouge

COACH: **JIM HASLETT**

2002 SAINTS: 9-7

DATE	OPPONENT	RESULT
Sept. 8	at Buccaneers	W 26-20
Sept. 15	Packers	W 35-20
Sept. 22	at Bears	W 29-23
Sept. 29	at Lions	L 26-21
Oct. 6	Steelers	W 32-29
Oct. 13	at Redskins	W 43-27
Oct. 20	49ers	W 35-27
Oct. 27	Falcons	L 37-35
Nov. 10	at Panthers	W 34-24
Nov. 17	at Falcons	L 24-17
Nov. 24	Browns	L 24-15
Dec. 1	Buccaneers	W 23-20
Dec. 8	at Ravens	W 37-25
Dec. 15	Vikings	L 32-31
Dec. 22	at Bengals	L 20-13
Dec. 29	Panthers	L 10-6

COACH: **JIM HASLETT**

2003 SAINTS: 8-8

DATE	OPPONENT	RESULT
Sept. 7	at Seahawks	L 27-10
Sept. 14	Texans	W 31-10
Sept. 21	at Titans	L 27-12
Sept. 28	Colts	L 55-21
Oct. 5	at Panthers	L 19-13
Oct. 12	Bears	W 20-13
Oct. 19	at Falcons	W 45-17
Oct. 26	Panthers	L 23-20 OT
Nov. 2	at Buccaneers	W 17-14
Nov. 16	Falcons	W 23-20 OT
Nov. 23	at Eagles	L 33-20
Nov. 30	at Redskins	W 24-20
Dec. 7	Buccaneers	L 14-7
Dec. 14	Giants	W 45-7
Dec. 21	at Jaguars	L 20-19
Dec. 28	Cowboys	W 13-7

COACH: **JIM HASLETT**

2004 SAINTS: 8-8

DATE	OPPONENT	RESULT
Sept. 12	Seahawks	L 21-7
Sept. 19	49ers	W 30-27
Sept. 26	at Rams	W 28-25 OT
Oct. 3	at Cardinals	L 34-10
Oct. 10	Buccaneers	L 20-17
Oct. 17	Vikings	L 38-31
Oct. 24	at Raiders	W 31-26
Nov. 7	at Chargers	L 43-17
Nov. 14	Chiefs	W 27-20
Nov. 21	Broncos	L 34-13
Nov. 28	at Falcons	L 24-21
Dec. 5	Panthers	L 32-21
Dec. 12	at Cowboys	W 27-13
Dec. 19	at Buccaneers	W 21-17
Dec. 26	Falcons	W 26-13
Jan. 2	at Panthers	W 21-18

COACH: **JIM HASLETT**

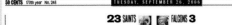

The Times-Picayune

23 SAINTS — **FALCONS 3**

WHAT A SHOW!

ELECTRIFYING SAINTS ROUT FALCONS; NOW 3-0

FANS, DOME, NEW ORLEANS SHINE ON NATIONAL STAGE

A president Larry Rolling says it all with his sign before the end of the game Monday. Police officers and other Superdome veterans at the game said the emotion was indescribable, like nothing they had ever seen, as raucous screams of "Who Dat!" reverberated through the Dome.

For Saints fans, an emotional return to a hurricane symbol

Crowd pushes enthusiasm to a higher level at Dome

Sept. 25, 2006

DREAMLAND

SAINTS' HISTORIC VICTORY PUTS THEM ONE WIN FROM THE SUPER BOWL

Jan. 13, 2007

The Saints' magical ride comes to an end in Chicago

THANK YOU, BOYS

Jan. 21, 2007

SPORTS

BABY BOOMERS

Young players deliver like veterans as Saints win Payton's debut

Sept. 10, 2006

SPORTS

TOUCHDOWN

Oct. 8, 2006

SPORTS

THE REAL DEAL

Saints rise to 5-1 with comeback that grounds high-flying Eagles

Oct. 15, 2006

SPORTS

BUSH BASH

Dec. 3, 2006

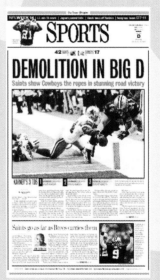

SPORTS

DEMOLITION IN BIG D

Saints show Cowboys the ropes in stunning road victory

Dec. 10, 2006

SPORTS

BYE IS NIGH

With visions of a week off in their heads, Saints hurdle Giants

Dec. 24, 2006